I0118928

Anonymous

Refunding of the National Debt

Anonymous

Refunding of the National Debt

ISBN/EAN: 9783744662468

Printed in Europe, USA, Canada, Australia, Japan

Cover: Foto ©Suzi / pixelio.de

More available books at **www.hansebooks.com**

REFUNDING OF THE NATIONAL DEBT.

NOTES

OF

AN INTERVIEW

BETWEEN

THE FINANCE COMMITTEE OF THE SENATE

AND

THE SECRETARY OF THE TREASURY, THE COMPTROLLER OF THE CURRENCY, AND THE TREASURER OF THE UNITED STATES,

WITH REGARD TO

THE BILL (H. R. 4592) TO FACILITATE THE REFUNDING OF THE NATIONAL DEBT.

WASHINGTON:
GOVERNMENT PRINTING OFFICE.
1881.

REFUNDING OF NATIONAL DEBT.

STATEMENTS

BEFORE THE

COMMITTEE ON FINANCE, UNITED STATES SENATE,

WITH REGARD TO

The bill (H. R. 4592) to facilitate the refunding of the national debt, in the following words :

[46th Congress, 3d Session. H. R. 4592.]

AN ACT to facilitate the refunding of the national debt.

Be it enacted by the Senate and House of Representatives of the United States of America in Congress assembled, That all existing provisions of law authorizing the refunding of the national debt shall apply to any bonds of the United States bearing a higher rate of interest than four and one-half per centum per annum which may hereafter become redeemable : *Provided,* That in lieu of the bonds authorized to be issued by the act of July fourteenth, eighteen hundred and seventy, entitled "An act to authorize the refunding of the national debt," and the acts amendatory thereto, and the certificates authorized by the act of February twenty-sixth, eighteen hundred and seventy-nine, entitled "An act to authorize the issue of certificates of deposit in aid of the refunding of the public debt," the Secretary of the Treasury is hereby authorized to issue bonds in the amount of not exceeding four hundred million dollars, which shall bear interest at the rate of three per centum per annum, redeemable, at the pleasure of the United States, after five years, and payable ten years from the date of issue, and also certificates in the amount of three hundred million dollars, in denominations of ten, twenty, and fifty dollars, either registered or coupon, bearing interest at the rate of three per centum per annum, redeemable, at the pleasure of the United States, after one year, and payable in ten years from the date of issue. The bonds and certificates shall be, in all other respects, of like character and subject to the same provisions as the bonds authorized to be issued by the act of July fourteenth, eighteen hundred and seventy, entitled "An act to authorize the refunding of the national debt," and acts amendatory thereto : *Provided,* That nothing in this act shall be so construed as to authorize an increase of the public debt : *Provided further,* That interest upon the six per cent. bonds hereby authorized to be refunded shall cease at the expiration of thirty days after notice that the same have been designated by the Secretary of the Treasury for redemption.

1 N D

SEC. 2. The Secretary of the Treasury is hereby authorized, in the process of refunding the national debt, to exchange, at not less than par, any of the bonds or certificates herein authorized for any of the bonds of the United States outstanding and uncalled bearing a higher rate of interest than four and one-half per centum per annum ; and on the bonds so redeemed the Secretary of the Treasury may allow to the holders the difference between the interest on such bonds from the date of exchange to the time of their maturity and the interest for a like period·on the bonds or certificates issued ; but none of the provisions of this act shall apply to the redemption or exchange of any of the bonds issued to the Pacific Railway Companies; and the bonds so received and exchanged in pursuance of the provisions of this act shall be canceled and destroyed.

SEC. 3. Authority to issue bonds and certificates to the amount necessary to carry out the provisions of this act is hereby granted; and the Secretary of the Treasury is hereby authorized and directed to make suitable rules and regulations to carry this act into effect: *Provided*, That the expense of preparing, issuing, advertising, and disposing of the bonds and certificates authorized to be issued shall not exceed one-quarter of one per centum.

SEC. 4. That the Secretary of the Treasury is hereby authorized, if in his opinion it shall become necessary, to use not exceeding fifty million dollars of the standard gold and silver coin in the Treasury in the redemption of the five and six per cent. bonds of the United States authorized to be refunded by the provisions of this act; and he may at any time apply the surplus money in the Treasury not otherwise appropriated, or so much thereof as he may consider proper, to the purchase or redemption of United States bonds or certificates: *Provided*, That the bonds and certificates so purchased or redeemed shall constitute no part of the sinking fund, but shall be canceled.

SEC. 5. From and after the first day of May, eighteen hundred and eighty-one, the three per centum bonds authorized by the first section of this act shall be the only bonds receivable as security for national-bank circulation, or as security for the safe-keeping and prompt payment of the public money deposited with such banks; but when any such bonds deposited for the purposes aforesaid shall be designated for purchase or redemption by the Secretary of the Treasury, the banking association depositing the same shall have the right to substitute other issues of the bonds of the United States in lieu thereof: *Provided*, That no bond upon which interest has ceased shall be accepted or shall be continued on deposit as security for circulation or for the safe-keeping of the public money; and in case bonds so deposited shall not be withdrawn, as provided by law, within thirty days after interest has ceased thereon, the banking association depositing the same shall be subject to the liabilities and proceedings on the part of the Comptroller provided for in section fifty-two hundred and thirty-four of the Revised Statutes of the United States : *And provided further,* That section four of the act of June twentieth, eighteen hundred and seventy-four, entitled, "An act fixing the amount of United States notes, providing for a redistribution of the national-bank currency, and for other purposes," be, and the same is hereby, repealed ; and sections fifty-one hundred and fifty-nine and fifty-one hundred and sixty of the Revised Statutes of the United States be, and the same are hereby, re enacted.

SEC. 6. That this act shall be known as " The funding act of eighteen hundred and eighty-one;" and all acts and parts of acts inconsistent with this act are hereby repealed.

TUESDAY, *January* 25, 1881.

Present, the members of the committee. Also, Hon. John Sherman, Secretary of the Treasury; Hon. J. K. Upton, Assistant Secretary of the Treasury; and Hon. John Jay Knox, Comptroller of the Currency.

The CHAIRMAN (Senator BAYARD). You will express to the committee, Mr. Secretary, your opinion of the bonds proposed in the first section of the bill under consideration.

Secretary SHERMAN. My attention has been called chiefly to three points in the bill : first, as to the rate of interest proposed; second, as to the appropriation for the expense of preparing and disposing of the bonds; and, third, as to the policy of the 5th section. Minor amendments suggest themselves, as, for instance, that a 5·20 bond would probably be better for some reasons; and I will add also that the denominations of the certificates should be increased so that they will be not less than $10 and multiples of that sum. The great body of these would be in smaller denominations, but it would be often convenient as the basis of call loans to have denominations of $100, $500, and $1,000, and perhaps higher denominations, and there could be no objection to their use. The word "certificates" does not convey the exact idea of the notes provided for, but the term "Treasury notes" is more in conformity with the laws of the United States heretofore providing for short loans.

As to the rate of interest proposed I can only say that I do not believe the loan proposed can be negotiated at 3 per cent. interest. I do not say that it cannot be, but that is my opinion, based mainly upon the fact that our bonds now in the market are selling at prices which yield more than 3 per cent. to the holders, showing that the borrowing power of the government is not so low as 3 per cent., and that no government has ever yet sold its bonds bearing 3 per cent. interest at par. Whenever bonds bearing that rate of interest have been offered they have been sold at enough less than par to produce to the investor about 3½ per cent. interest as a minimum. To ascertain this fact the Treasury Department obtained from several foreign governments the rates at which their loans had been disposed of, and I have tables based upon this information, some of the most important of which I will furnish to the committee. The first one in reference to Great Britain shows only transactions in recent unfunded loans. It will be observed that all the exchequer bills mentioned in the following statement bear rate of interest from 2 to 3½ per cent., run for a short time, and were issued when the money market was easy, and they are in the nature of money. The aggregate amount, about $100,000,000, would be available for current uses, and. the loans could not have been extended to any large sum at such rates.

A full statement of the bonded loans of that country may be found on page 110, Finance Report for 1879.

Statement of the unfunded debt of Great Britain on the 31st of March, 1880.

(Prepared for the purpose of answering certain questions of the American Government.)

Character of obligation.	Amount.	Date of maturity.	Rate of interest.	When and at what rate issued.	Market value, March 31, 1880, exclusive of accrued interest.
Exchequer bonds	£3,200,000	Various dates in 1880	2¼ %	At par, 1879	Not on market.
Do	3,901,100	Payable half-yearly up to 1912	3½ %	At par, 1876	Do.
Do	8,750,000	Various dates from March, 1881, to March, 1883	3¼ %	At par, on various dates between March, 1878, and March, 1880.	Do.
Treasury bills	1,461,000	Due six months from date of issue	£2 5s. 10d.	Issued at par	No quotation.
Do	3,950,000	Due three months from date of issue	2 3s.	do	do.
Exchequer bills	2,535,800	June, 1881	2 %	Issued at par in June, 1876	4s. discount to 1s. premium.
Do	100	June, 1866	Not bearing interest.	Issued at par in 1861	
Do	1,471,300	March, 1882	2¼ %	£1,329,700 issued at par, and £98,600 issued at prices varying from 7s. to 12s., premium in March, 1877.	Par to 4s. premium.
Do	464,400	do	2¼ %	Issued at 1s. premium in March, 1878	Do.
Do	665,200	do	2¼ %	Issued at 4s. premium in March, 1879	Do.
Do	26,000	do	2¼ %	Issued at 1s. premium in March, 1880	Do.
Advance by Bank of England in aid of ways and means.	1,000,000				
	27,344,900				

The market rate of three per cent. interest has practically never existed in England, as will be seen from the following paragraph from the London Economist:

In 1852 consols were quoted at prices varying from 3 below par to nearly 102; the history of matters for that year being as follows: Consols rose from 97 ex div. in January and touched 100 in May, and 101 early in June. They were then quoted ex div., but were again quoted at 101 ex div. on the 23d of June. Best bills were at that time taken in the open market at 1¼ per cent. During August there was a relapse to 99¼. But at the beginning of September consols were again above 100. They remained about that price until November, when they rose to 101¼, and in December to 101⅞, They were then quoted 100¼ ex div., but closed for the year at 101 ex div. In 1853 from 101 they fell below 100 in the first fortnight in January, and reduced 3 per cents, then at 101¼, quickly followed. But in March they recovered to 100, and towards the end of April they rose to 101. Consols relapsed to 100 in June, and were then quoted 98½ ex div. They were as low as 90 in October, 1853, and have not since been at par until November, 1880.—*London Economist, November* 6, 1880.

The table in regard to France embraces all the loans of that country from 1816 to 1880. I have no information of any loan in France since the popular loans from 1870 to 1872, which was taken by public subscription. It will be noticed that in 1863 the French 3 per cents were sold by public subscription at 66.30. In 1868 the same class of securities was sold by public subscription at 69.25. In 1870 the 3 per cents were sold by public subscription at 60.60. The 5 per cents in 1871, immediately after the Prussian war, were sold at 82.50 in very large sums, and in 1872 at 84.50.

The statement of French loans is as follows:

Laws authorizing the loans.	Dates of negotiation.	Kind of rentes. Per ct.	Amount of rentes. Francs.	Rate of the negotiation. Francs.	Proceeds of loans. Francs.	Manner of negotiation.
Law of April 28, 1816, art. 117	May 1, 1816 / April 1, 1817	5	6,000,000	57.26 Average price.	69,763,000	At home and abroad.
Law of April 25, 1817	1817 and 1818	5	30,000,000	57.51 Average price.	345,065,000	French and foreign companies. Negotiations at home.
Law of May 6 and 15, 1818	May 9, 1818	5	14,925,500	66.50	197,909,040	Different subscribers.
Law of May 6, 1818	Octo. 9, 1818	5	12,313,433	67.00	165,000,000	Hope & Co. and Baring Bros. & Co.
Law of May 6 and 15, 1818, and of March 8, 1821	Aug. 9, 1821	5	9,585,220	85.55	164,003,114	Hottingner & Co., Hope & Co., Bagueault & Co., Delessert & Co. (Adjudication.)
Law of 1821, 1822, and 1823	July 10 1823	5	23,114,516	89.55	413,960,981	Rothschild Bros. (Adjudication.)
Law of June 19, 1828	Jan. 12, 1830	4	3,134,050	102.07½	80,000,005	Idem.
			93,073,619		1,435,721,140	
Law of March 25, 1831	April 19, 1831	5	7,142,858	84.00	120,000.014	Different bankers and receivers-general. (Adjudication.)
Law of April 21 1831	Nat. loan, 1831	5	1,021,945	par.	20,438,900	Different subscribers.
Law of 1831 and April 21, 1832	Aug. 8, 1832	5	7,614,213	98.50	150,000,000	Rothschild, Davilliers & Hottingner. (Adjudication.)
Law of June 25, 1841	Oct. 18, 1841	3	5,730,659	78.52⅜	130,000,000	Rothschild Bros., Hottingner, London, Saint-Didier and receivers-general. (Adjudication.)
Law of June 25, 1841	Dec. 9, 1844	3	7,079,646	84.75	200,000,000	Rothschild Bros. (Adjudication.)
Law of August 8, 1847	Nov. 10, 1847	3	2,569,413 A	75.25	64,149,443	Idem.
			31,158,734		704,888,357	
Laws of March 31, 1839, and June 26, 1847	Savings-bank funds	4	8,092,647	par.	202,316,175	Account current of savings banks.
Decree of March 9, 1848	National loan, 1848	5	1,309,104	par.		
Decree of July 7, Aug. 9, and Nov. 21, 1848	Compensation to the subscribers of the National loan.	5	519,283	Recalled by the compensation at 71.60	26,162,213.00	Different subscribers. Account of 1850, page 454.

	Date of issue	Rate	Amount	Price of issue	Amount realized	Observations
Decree of July 24, 1848	July 25, 1848	5	13,107,000	75.25	197,960,350.00	Rentes attributed to holders of certificates of the loan of 1847.
			14,935,387		223,442,563.00	
Law of March 11, 1854	March, 1854	4½	4,550,640	92.50	93,540,933.00	⎫
		3	7,159,390	65.25	155,721,062.50	⎪
Law of Dec. 31, 1854	Jan'y, 1855	4½	8,052,120	92.00	164,691,190.00	⎪
		3	15,857,530	65.25	344,901,277.50	⎬ Public subscriptions.
Law of July 11, 1855	July, 1855	4½	4,389,760	92.25	89,990,080.00	⎪
		3	31,699,740	65.25	659,469,345.00	⎪
Law of May 2, 1859	May, 1859	4½	573,710	90.00	11,474,200.00	⎪
		3	25,199,660	60.50	508,193,143.33	⎭
Law of 1855 and 1857	1857, 1858, 1859, 1860, and 1861.	3	7,942,315	Various rates; average, 69.10	182,947,676.00	Consolidation of the funds of the Army endowment.
Law of June 9, 1857	Dec. 31, 1859.	3	4,000,000	75.00	100,000,000.00	Treaty with the Bank of France.
Law of February 12, 1862	1862; conversion of 30-year obligations.	3	12,092,520	66.49 Average.	266,000,000.00	Approximate result of various rates of issues of obligations, (p. 434 of the Account of 1862.) (443 fr. 25 c. average for 504, 626 obligations.)
Law of December 30, 1863	Jan., 1864	3	14,240,339	66.30	314,910,391.90	Public subscription.
Law of August 1, 1868	Aug., 1868	3	19,514,315	69.25	420,456,720.32	Idem.
Law of August 2, 1868	1869	3	4,000,000	par.	"	Conversion of Mexican bonds.
Law of August 12, 1870	1870	3	39,890,306	60.60	804,572,181.20	Public subscription.
			199,111,545		4,178,798,150.75	
Law of June 21, 1871	1871	5	138,975,295	82.50	2,293,092,367.50	Public subscription.
Law of July 15, 1872	1872	5	207,026,310	84.50	3,498,744,639.00	Public subscription.
			346,001,605		5,791,837,006.50	

A. Part realized by the loan of 250 millions, authorized in 1847.

TREASURY DEPARTMENT *January* 21, 1860.

The interest on the French securities at the present market rates would yield the investor about $4\frac{1}{4}$ per cent.

In regard to the German loans, here is a table which shows the bonds negotiated by Germany in 1878, 1879, and 1880. Those are all 4 per cent. bonds. They sold from 96 to $100\frac{3}{4}$. The average rate of interest to the purchaser was $4\frac{18}{100}$.

Senator KERNAN. What was the time of the bonds?

Secretary SHERMAN. Those, I think, are annuities, but I am not sure. They follow the English plan, I think.

The CHAIRMAN. Not a short loan?

Secretary SHERMAN. A long loan. I think it is an annuity.

Statement of bonds negotiated by Germany in 1878 and 1879, compiled from official informa- tion received at the United States Treasury Department.

	Nominal val- ue (marks).	Rate realized.	Amount real- ized (marks).	Average rate of interest to pur- chaser.
To September, 1879 .... 4 %	167, 866, 700	98. 749 %	160, 100, 177 45	
October, 1879 .... 4 %	1, 059, 800	98¼ and 98. 60 %	1, 042, 889	
October and November,1879 4 %	30, 000, 000	96 %	28, 755, 000	
January 31, 1880 .... 4 %	8, 290, 300	97¼ to 100¼ %	8, 114, 783 55	
Total (marks)................	207, 216, 800	Average...95. 558 %	198, 012, 850	4. 18 %

TREASURY DEPARTMENT, *January* 22, 1880.

Secretary SHERMAN. In regard to the rates in this country, here is a table, which is cut from a public document, showing the rates at which the United States loans were placed on the market, with the cal- culated rates of interest realized to investors, at different periods from 1796 to 1861. The loans since that time we could not compare very well, because they were sold for paper money at a discount, but if de- sired we can give you the rates realized to investors. The lowest point which interest ever reached in this country prior to 1879, say, was in 1824 and along there, when they were refunding a portion of the old Revolutionary stock. From 1821 to 1824 they sold 5 per cents at a premium of $5\frac{1}{10}$ to 8, and $4\frac{1}{2}$'s in sums of about $5,000,000 a year at par.

Senator FERRY. How much premium was realized on the 5 per cents?

Secretary SHERMAN. The 5 per cents sold for from $5\frac{1}{10}$ to 8 per cent. premium, and they then withdrew the 5's and put on the $4\frac{1}{2}$'s.

Senator KERNAN. You say about $5,000,000 a year?

Secretary SHERMAN. Never more than $5,000,000 a year.

Senator FERRY. What was the necessity for it?

Secretary SHERMAN. Partly to meet the payments of certain awards to Spain, and partly for the refunding of a 6 per cent. debt. This ran for 8, 9, or 10 years, and it was finally paid off during the administra- tion of General Jackson.

to 1861, inclusive.

[Prepared in the office of the Secretary of the Treasury.]

Year placed on market.	Title of loan.	Rate of interest.	Amount issued.	Price of sale.	Years to run.	Rate realized to investors.
		Per cent.		*Per cent.*		*Per cent.*
1796	Six per cent. stock of 1796	6	$80,000 00	87½	24	7.09
1798	Eight per cent. stock of 1798	8	5,000,000 00	Par.	15	8
1800	Eight per cent. stock of 1800	8	1,481,700 00	105.64	15	7.37
1807	Exchanged six per cent. stock of 1807	6	6,294,051 12	Par.	Indefinite.	6
1812	Six per cent. stock of 1812	6	8,134,700 00	Par.	13	6
1812	Exchanged six per cent. stock of 1812	6	*2,984,746 72	Par.	13	6
1813	Sixteen million loan of 1813	6	*18,109,377 43	88	13	7.54
1813	Seven and one-half million loan of 1813	6	4,427,575 07	88.25	12	7.50
1814	Seven and one-half million loan of 1813	6	4,071,008 50	88.25	12	7.50
1814	Ten million loan of 1814	6	9,919,476 25	80	12	8.72
1814	Six million loan of 1814	6	5,384,134 87	80	12	8.72
1814	Undesignated loan of 1814	6	157,694 68	95	11	8.51
1815	Undesignated loan of 1814	6	147,058 81	85	11	8.08
1815	Undesignated loan of 1814	6	47,627 79	90.75	11	7.90
1815	Undesignated loan of 1814	6	82,480 72	90.50	11	7.90
1816	Undesignated loan of 1814	6	18,600 00	85	10	8.08
1816	Undesignated loan of 1814	6	87,912 06	91	10	7.92
1816	Undesignated loan of 1814	6	904,989 23	80	10	9.09
1821	Five per cent. stock of 1821	5	4,735,296 30	5.1 @ 8 prm.	13 5/16	4.22
1824	Four and one-half per cent. stock of 1824, act of May 24, 1824	4½	5,000,000 00	Par.	8	4½
1824	Exchanged four and one-half per cent. stock of 1824	4½	4,454,727 95	Par.	8 and 9	4½
1824	Four and one-half per cent. stock of 1824, act of May 26, 1824	4½	5,000,000 00	Par.	Indefinite.	4½
1825	Exchanged four and one-half per cent. stock of 1825	4½	1,539,336 16	Par.	3 and 4	4½
1842	Loan of 1842	5	8,343,886 03	97.50 to par.	20	6 to 6.22
1843	Loan of 1843	5	7,004,231 35	1 to 3.75 prm.	10	4.52 to 4.87
1846	Loan of 1846	6	4,999,149 45	Par.	10	6
1847	Loan of 1847	6	28,207,000 00	1.25 @ 2 prm.	20	5.89 to 5.89
1848	Loan of 1848	6	16,000,000 00	3.02 @ 4 prm.	20	5.66 to 5.74
1858	Loan of 1858	5	20,000,000 00	Par.	15	5
1861	Loan of February, 1861	6	18,415,000 00	89.03	10 or 20	7.59 to 7.03
1861	Loan of July and August, 1861	6	189,321,200 00	97.18	20	6.25

*The amount of cash received on the loan was $16,000,000; of which amount $331,200 was placed at *par* with an annuity of 1¼ per cent., making the interest realized on the sixteen millions 7.50 per cent.

As to the interest in New York at this time, which is an indication also, I have a table taken from the report of the Comptroller of the Currency, which Mr. Knox furnishes me. This is on call loans and on commercial paper, together with the average rate of discount in the Bank of England for the same time, showing the rates of interest. That probably would be better as an element of computation.

*The average rate of interest in New York City for each of the fiscal years from 1874 to 1880, as ascertained from data derived from the Journal of Commerce and The Commercial and Financial Chronicle, was as follows:

1874, call loans, 3. 8 per cent. ; commercial paper, 6. 4 per cent.
1875, call loans, 3. 0 per cent. ; commercial paper, 5. 6 per cent.
1876, call loans, 3. 3 per cent. ; commercial paper, 5. 3 per cent.
1877, call loans, 3. 0 per cent. ; commercial paper, 5. 2 per cent.
1878, call loans, 4. 4 per cent. ; commercial paper, 5. 1 per cent.
1879, call loans, 4. 4 per cent. ; commercial paper, 4. 4 per cent.
1880, call loans, 4. 9 per cent. ; commercial paper, 5. 3 per cent.
Calendar year 1880, call loans, 3. 8 per cent.; commercial paper, 4. 7 per cent.

The average rate of discount of the Bank of England for the same years was as follows:

During the calendar year ending December 31, 1874, 3. 69 per cent.
During the calendar year ending December 31, 1875, 3. 23 per cent.
During the calendar year ending December 31, 1876, 2. 61 per cent.
During the calendar year ending December 31, 1877, 2. 91 per cent.
During the calendar year ending December 31, 1878, 3. 78 per cent.
During the calendar year ending December 31, 1879, 2. 50 per cent.
During the fiscal year ending June 30, 1880, 2. 63 per cent.

I wish to say that I have no doubt a portion of the Treasury notes, especially those which run a short time, can be sold as low as 3 per cent., and, therefore, I suggest, in addition to the amendments to the bill noted here, that if you should adopt the rate of 3½ for the certificates, or notes, it might be made "not to exceed 3½," because I have no doubt that a short loan might be made at 3 per cent., or possibly less, judging from the English experience. They sold 2½ per cent. short-time notes, similar to those provided by this bill, at par at a time when money was lying idle. Investment in these short-time obligations was like having money on call. They did sell these 2½ per cent. notes at par; but they were either for 3 or 6 months; but I am inclined to think we could sell one-year Treasury notes, especially if our surplus revenue makes it a certainty they will be redeemed at maturity. I should think there might be a time when they would sell with a lower rate than 3 per cent.

Senator VOORHEES. I wish to ask a question for information, Mr. Secretary. Why would a short investment be preferable to a long one? Why can we secure an investment for a short time in these Treasury notes at a less rate of interest than for a long run?

Secretary SHERMAN. The reason is that a call loan realizes always the lowest rate of interest, because the creditor can take all the advantages of the market. If there is a small rise, he makes his call and gets a larger rate of interest.

Senator VOORHEES. This would be, then, like an operation in the streets or in the banks, while the other would bear the features of a permanent investment.

Senator FERRY. In that connection, I see your surplus of 1880 is $65,000,000.

Secretary SHERMAN. Yes; I suppose you have the table.

Senator FERRY. And your sinking fund of 1880 is $40,000,000.

Secretary SHERMAN. That is part of the $65,000,000.

Senator FERRY. I mean your requirement is $40,000,000. You have

---

*Report of the Comptroller of the Currency for the year 1880, page 55.

provided more than that, because it has been done before. With your surplus of some sixty-odd million dollars, could you not place at least $200,000,000 very readily? Your sinking fund would require in 5 years $200,000,000.

Secretary SHERMAN. I have no doubt we can sell some notes. I have been quite in favor of trying these short-time Treasury notes; I recommended them in my Report.

Senator WALLACE. Does the bill contain any provision by which these may be held by banks as a part of the surplus?

Secretary SHERMAN. They are held like bills discounted.

Senator WALLACE. Could they be held as greenbacks?

Secretary SHERMAN. No, sir; they ought to be held only like any other short loan.

Senator KERNAN. Would they circulate?

Secretary SHERMAN. For a few days they might circulate, but not much. They would be held like a call loan.

Senator VOORHEES. You say the Treasury notes will not go a great deal into circulation?

Secretary SHERMAN. I do not think they will to any great extent. They might for a little while, when the coupons are just cut off. After that, every man will hold them in preference to currency, because they are a little better than currency, as they would draw interest.

Senator MORRILL. What do you think about having any surplus in the face of the statement of Commissioner of Pensions Bentley that the arrears of pensions act is going to cost $521,000,000?

Secretary SHERMAN. I take it Congress will manage that matter. I want to say as a fact that we have already paid out all of the money appropriated for the fiscal year for pensions. I have stated it, and I state it to you now. It is a question seriously to consider, that there is an estimate before you of $19,000,000 deficiency for pensions. We have already paid the entire annual appropriation.

Senator KERNAN. Up to June next?

Secretary SHERMAN. Up to June next; and there is a deficiency asked for.

Senator KERNAN. For this year?

Secretary SHERMAN. For this year; and it is a pretty serious matter. That cuts $19,000,000 off of the $50,000,000 surplus we were to have this year, according to the Treasury estimates submitted in my annual Report.

Senator FERRY. Our excess of imports over exports for the first six months of last year was $63,000,000, and for the last five months it was $53,000,000.

Senator BECK. Mr. Secretary, I do not want to interrupt you, but wish you to get your tables in as rapidly as possible.

Secretary SHERMAN. I should like to do so. I would state that I have another table here which I think will be of value, and you will find it so when you come to study this matter. It shows the market value of a 3 per cent. bond at the present market rate. I think it is the same table that Senator FERRY has. It shows that a bond placed below the normal rate gradually runs down in value according to the period it has to run. A bond for $100 for one year at 3 per cent. will be worth $99.76, and will gradually run down until, if payable at the end of fifty years, its present worth will be only $93.80. Its value will never reach par so long as the interest it bears is below the market rate yielded by other United States bonds.

This is the table:

Table showing the net value of a three per cent. bond, interest reinvested semi-annually to run 1, 2, 3, 4, 5, 6, 7, 8, 9, 10, 15, 20, 30, and 50 years to payment, and of a three per cent. perpetuity (or perpetual annuity), computed on the basis of the present net prices in open market of the United States four per cent. securities redeemable in 1907, at which rate investors will realize 3¼ per cent. interest per annum.

	Corresponding net price of 3 per cent. bonds.
Years to run to payment: 1	99.76
2	99.50
3	99.30
4	99.10
5	98.90
6	98.60
7	98.50
8	98.30
9	98.10
10	97.90
15	97.05
20	96.30
30	95.20
50	93.80
Perpetuity	92.30

TREASURY DEPARTMENT,
January 21, 1881.

Then, again, if you issue a 3 per cent. bond you would have to abandon the established policy of this country, which has always been to maintain its bonds at par. Ever since the scheme of Hamilton, it has been the policy of the government to maintain its bonds at par, and not adopt the English system, to sell bonds bearing a fixed rate of interest at any price they would bring. Congress has always tenaciously held to the idea that the securities of the United States should be of such a character as would bring par. If, then, 3¼ per cent. is the normal minimum rate of interest, the issue of bonds that would be continued below par would be a departure from that policy, and, besides that, it would impair the fund for the security of the note-holders in the banking system, and would compel the Comptroller of the Currency, as soon as this deficiency appears, to require the difference to be made good by additional bonds.

Senator FERRY. Is there not a ten per cent. margin already?

Secretary SHERMAN. Yes; but the Comptroller has got to keep that. The Senator seems to fall into the impression that the 3 per cent. 10 or 20 year bond would be quoted the first year at 99.76. That is not it. The table is made upon the idea that the bond is to be a 3 per cent. one-year bond, which would only be quoted at 99.76.

Senator KERNAN. Not for one year of ten?

Secretary SHERMAN. No; but if it was issued running for ten years, then, as a matter of course, its value would depend upon the rate of interest it would yield within the ten years, and this value would be $97.90 for $100. I have here also a table that has been prepared by Mr. Elliott. This is a table for a 3½ per cent. bond upon the assumption that 3¼ per cent. is the par. That is, the 3½ per cent. bond would be of higher value depending upon its duration. The bond would increase in value the longer it runs.

Senator ALLISON. As the number of years increases?

Secretary SHERMAN. As the number of years increases. If you would make it a five-year bond, it might be fairly quoted and sold at a little above par.

Senator VOORHEES. You speak of 3¼ per cent. being the rate of interest on a par bond?

Secretary SHERMAN. The minimum rate.

Senator VOORHEES. Does the element of the time which the bond has to run have anything to do with that in your statement, or do you speak of a one-year bond or a two year bond or a bond of any length of time making that rate?

Secretary SHERMAN. As a rule, call loans can be put at the lowest rate of interest, and perhaps the rate can be kept down if payment is to be made within a year or so, but when the time is so long that the loan becomes desirable as an investment, then, if the rate of interest is good, the loan becomes more valuable the longer time it has to run; but if the annual interest yield is lower than the market rate, the converse of this statement will be true.

Senator VOORHEES. If you are throwing a loan upon the money markets of the world, do you say the short bond would be most valuable? Could you sell the short bonds in larger amount?

Secretary SHERMAN. A bond payable in one year, I think, would be sold at a better rate to a certain limited amount.

Senator VOORHEES. But not to such a large amount?

Secretary SHERMAN. No; because this bill does not anticipate, I imagine, that we shall force the bonds on the market. You can put them on the market only to the extent of the demand for them for convenient use in the nature of call loans. Last fall we could have sold a large amount of such bonds, for the reason that gold was pouring into the country and holders could realize hardly anything from it. We could have paid for this gold with great advantage with one-year Treasury notes, which could have been used in the nature of currency, and could have used the gold in the redemption of higher-rate securities of the United States.

Senator KERNAN. Of one-year bonds?

Secretary SHERMAN. Of one-year bonds.

Senator FERRY. Simply to invest the surplus money?

Secretary SHERMAN. Simply to invest the surplus money.

Senator VOORHEES. Do I understand that you have serious objection to this 5-10 bond? I have understood that the capital of the country is opposed to that provision because it is too short a bond.

Secretary SHERMAN. No; I think not. I think the right of the United States to redeem its securities is a very important right. That right I would not surrender. Therefore I am in favor of the 5-20 bond. I would make it a 5-20 bond because that does not deprive the United States of the right of redemption after five years, and gives an appearance of permanency, and, besides, it is the title of a bond to which the people have become accustomed.

Senator BECK. There is another element in that, too—that $250,000,000 of 4½ per cent. bonds mature in 1891.

Secretary SHERMAN. Yes; that is important. We cannot, with the sinking fund, pay off all these bonds in ten years. I think we shall have to reserve the right to let some of them run twenty years. It does us no harm, because we can pay them at the end of five years if we have a surplus revenue.

Senator FERRY. It gives you command of the situation.

Secretary SHERMAN. It gives us command of the situation.

Senator FERRY. You pay in twenty years if not before? You have the right of redemption in ten years?

Secretary SHERMAN. If you make this a 5-10 bond, the loan would mature and have to be paid at the very time the 4½ per cents mature, and we might get ourselves into a corner.

Senator VOORHEES. I have an impression that one of the objections to a short bond, a 5-10 bond, in such large amounts, is that it would not permanently fix itself as an investment; for instance, take large estates, or take men who have retired from business with millions of dollars that they want to put away; they would not wish to be disturbed again in the course of five or ten years; they would prefer a more permanent investment than that. I am very glad to hear you say that you think a bond at 3½ even could be floated. The extension of from ten to twenty years is not, I think, of so much importance. The privilege already of the government to commence at five years, if we have the surplus to use it and pay it, is an important privilege.

Senator KERNAN. As I understand the Secretary, in his judgment we should be able to negotiate a 5-10 bond at 3½ per cent.?

Secretary SHERMAN. Yes; I think a 3½ per cent. bond, running for five years, would sell at par.

Senator FERRY. As your sinking fund is forty-odd millions of dollars, and there is more or less surplus money that wants to be invested, which meets the point made by Senator Voorhees, that there is a great deal of idle money that men would like to invest, with that surplus money and the demand of the sinking fund at forty-odd millions, can you not place $250,000,000 at 3 per cent.?

Secretary SHERMAN. You cannot tell what the surplus revenue will be. It is true that all the money you mention may be seeking investment, but purchasers will take the best investment in the market. If railroads or other securities will pay a greater interest than government securities, investment will be made in them. Large portions of these sums would probably be invested in government securities, but, if so, it would be in those that can be bought the cheapest and yield the highest rate of interest. At present, any of the other government bonds at market rates will pay a higher rate of interest than three per cent. There would be no object in the holders of such funds purchasing three per cent. bonds. You must offer a bond that is as good in the market as other government bonds, or you cannot expect to sell. No one knows how many of the small notes would be absorbed. It may be $50,000,000; it may be more; but your real reliance must be upon the bonds that are offered.

Senator MORRILL. If you do not have a repetition of the year 1879, and the tremendous speculation in New York should result in a revulsion, so that the market was changed, would not that make some difference in the negotiation of any large loan?

Secretary SHERMAN. There might be some revulsion. I always speak of the present favorable condition of affairs. If you do not avail yourself of this, I cannot foresee the result.

Senator BECK. Before you leave this particular point—the bill passed by the House provides that the bonds and certificates to be issued "shall be in all other respects of like character and subject to the same provisions as the bonds authorized to be issued by the act of July 14, 1870, entitled 'An act to authorize the refunding of the national debt, and acts amendatory thereto.'" The provisions of all these laws require you to give 90 days' notice before you can pay off any of the bonds issued under them. Why should we not in issuing these new bonds so far modify the law as to authorize them to be paid upon 30 days' notice?

Secretary SHERMAN. There is no objection to that.

Senator BECK. Unless you desire to retain that privilege, I want to know why we should not make it 30 days.

The CHAIRMAN. Would not the proviso from line 31 to line 35 repeal that?

Senator FERRY. That applies to the interest on the 6 per cent. bonds.

Secretary SHERMAN. This is provided for by a substitute I have prepared for section 5, providing that, when these bonds are called, there shall be but one month's notice to holders.

Senator BECK. Why would it not be well after line 29 to insert the words "except it shall be paid after notice of thirty days," instead of ninety days, as now provided?

Secretary SHERMAN. Precisely; that we have got here at a different place.

Senator BECK. You propose to amend that?

Secretary SHERMAN. Yes.

Senator BECK. I beg pardon.

Secretary SHERMAN. This is the table showing the net value of a *three and a half* per cent. bond, interest reinvested semi-annually, to run 1, 2, 3, 4, 5, 6, 7, 8, 9, 10, 15, 20, 30, and 50 years to payment, and of $3\frac{1}{2}$ per cent. perpetuities (or perpetual annuities), computed on the basis of the present net prices in open market of the U. S. *four* per cent. consols of 1907:

Years to run to payment.	Corresponding net price of $3\frac{1}{2}$ per cent. bonds.
1	100.24
2	100.48
3	100.71
4	100.93
5	101.15
6	101.35
7	101.55
8	101.75
9	101.9
10	102.1
15	102.9
20	103.7
30	104.8
50	106.2
Perpetuity	107.7

E. B. ELLIOTT.

TREASURY DEPARTMENT,
Washington, D. C., January 24, 1881.

NOTE.—The rate of interest realized to investors in the *four* per cent. bonds, at present prices, on the assumption that the bonds will be paid as soon as redeemable, is *three and a fourth* per cent. per annum.

I have another table here which I think would be interesting to you, and it is an answer to some arguments made in the House. I do not know that I am at liberty here to talk of what was done in the House, but I suppose the committee can. Mr. Kelley, with a good deal of ingenuity, endeavored to show that it was not our interest to refund now, but we should, leaving the 5 or 6 per cent. bonds outstanding, just go on and pay them from the surplus revenue. In order to ascertain whether that was practical or not, I had this computation very carefully made. This shows the amount of interest we would be required to pay on the 5 and 6 per cent. bonds if they were retired at the rate of $50,000,000 per year, and that is what is proposed; and also another column showing the amount of interest to be paid on them if retired at the rate of $100,000,000 a year. It shows that we would pay on 5 and 6 per cent. bonds, if they were not refunded, but redeemed at the rate he proposes of $50,000,000 a year, $232,500,000 in interest. If paid off at the rate of $100,000,000 a year, it would be $125,500,000. If these bonds are refunded at $3\frac{1}{2}$ per cent., and redeemed at the rate of $50,000,000 a year, we would pay $159,250,000 for interest.

Senator VOORHEES. At $50,000,000 a year, commencing five years from now ?

Secretary SHERMAN. No, from this time on.

Senator VOORHEES. Please repeat the last statement.

Secretary SHERMAN. I say, if you authorize the 3½ per cent. bond as proposed in case the bill is amended, and apply $50,000,000 annually to redemptions, we would have paid in interest before they are all redeemed $159,250,000, which is about $80,000,000 less than we would pay under Mr. Kelley's plan. But if we redeem at the rate of $100,000,000 per annum we would only pay $87,750,000, or about $40,000,000 less. I suppose his argument, to state it fairly, would be that we ought not to issue bonds that could not be refunded and paid off at the proper time, and in that I agree with him, but we ought to refund, saving the right to redeem in short periods.

The CHAIRMAN. He has borne in mind nothing but the aggregation of interest. That was his theory.

Secretary SHERMAN. If the bill is passed as it came from the House, and we could by a possibility sell those bonds at par, the amount of interest we would pay at 3 per cent., supposing the redemptions to be made at the rate of $50,000,000 a year, would be $136,500,000, about $20,000,000 of interest less during the whole period than on the scale of 3½ per cent.

Senator KERNAN. You would save $20,000,000 of interest.

Secretary SHERMAN. We might save $20,000,000 of interest at 3 per cent., but at the same time in negotiating your bonds, in the delay and procrastination in the sale of those bonds, we would very probably lose all or more than we might save by the difference. As a matter of course any Secretary would desire to sell bonds at 3 per cent., and I think some certificates can be sold at that rate, but it may be a serious matter if we fail in this negotiation and have to go back to Congress for power to refund at a higher rate.

The statement of interest payments on the various bonds is as follows :

Statement showing interest payments required on three, three and a half, five, and six per cent. bonds for various periods.

	Five and six per cent. bonds continued, to be redeemed fifty millions per year.*	Five and six per cent. bonds continued and redeemed at rate of one hundred millions per year.*	Refunded at three and a half per cent, and redeemed at rate of fifty millions per year.	Refunded at three and a half per cent, and redeemed at rate of one hundred millions per year.	Refunded at three per cent., and redeemed at rate of fifty millions per year.	Refunded at three per cent, and redeemed at rate of one hundred millions per year.†
First year	$34,500,000	$34,500,000	$22,750,000	$22,750,000	$19,500,000	$19,500,000
Second year	31,500,000	28,500,000	21,000,000	19,250,000	18,000,000	16,500,000
Third year	28,500,000	22,500,000	19,250,000	15,750,000	16,500,000	13,500,000
Fourth year	25,500,000	17,500,000	17,500,000	12,250,000	15,000,000	10,500,000
Fifth year	22,500,000	12,500,000	15,750,000	8,750,000	13,500,000	7,500,000
Sixth year	20,000,000	7,500,000	14,000,000	5,250,000	12,000,000	4,500,000
Seventh year	17,500,000	2,500,000	12,250,000	1,750,000	10,500,000	1,500,000
Eighth year	15,000,000		10,500,000		9,000,000	
Ninth year	12,500,000		8,750,000		7,500,000	
Tenth year	10,000,000		7,000,000		6,000,000	
Eleventh year	7,500,000		5,250,000		4,500,000	
Twelfth year	5,000,000		3,500,000		3,000,000	
Thirteenth year	2,500,000		1,750,000		1,500,000	
Fourteenth year						
Total	232,500,000	125,500,000	159,250,000	85,750,000	136,500,000	73,500,000

* Assuming that the six per cent. bonds would be redeemed first and that the amount of bonds at the beginning was $650,000,000.

† Only three hundred millions could be redeemed in the first five years under present bill.

Senator KERNAN. When you come to that point, state to us why it would not be wise to say that the Secretary shall negotiate at a rate not exceeding 3½ per cent.

Senator VOORHEES. Making the rate not exceeding 3½ per cent. fixes it practically at that rate; you will not sell for less than that?

Secretary SHERMAN. No, it does not fix it. The same discretion would remain as in 1877, in the 4½ per cent. bonds.

Senator MORRILL. You stopped the sale of those?

Senator FERRY. Did that not show that the judgment of Congress did not meet the possibilities of the market?

Secretary SHERMAN. It showed then; but it does not follow because you could sell at 4 per cent., you can reduce it down.

Senator FERRY. But that being the case in that instance, where there were 5's and 4½'s and 4's, the result was, that your judgment moved you to arrest the sale of the 5's and 4½'s and confine yourself to the 4's. In view of the fact that your sinking fund requires forty odd million dollars a year, which in five years would absorb $200,000,000, and then considering the surplus money that wants to be placed in these low-rate bonds, simply on call, now with $200,000,000, say, that you have already, if such could be placed at 3 per cent. on short time, on what length of time can the balance of the $700,000,000 be placed at 3 per cent., in your judgment, over the $200,000,000? There is no question about the $200,000,000.

Senator KERNAN. I suggest to the Senator to let the Secretary get down with his tables to section 5.

Secretary SHERMAN. I will give another table bearing on the same question. In referring to the sinking fund, I produce this table for the purpose of showing how rapidly the requirements of the sinking fund would pay off the debt, and how important it is to have our bonds in reach so that we would not have to pay premium.

Requirements of the sinking fund for 10 years.

For the fiscal year ending June 30, 1882	$43,396,645 00
For the fiscal year ending June 30, 1883	45,122,110 80
For the fiscal year ending June 30, 1884	46,926,995 24
For the fiscal year ending June 30, 1885	48,804,075 04
For the fiscal year ending June 30, 1886	50,756,238 04
For the fiscal year ending June 30, 1887	52,786,487 56
For the fiscal year ending June 30, 1888	54,897,947 07
For the fiscal year ending June 30, 1889	57,093,864 95
For the fiscal year ending June 30, 1890	59,377,619 55
For the fiscal year ending June 30, 1891	61,752,724 33
	520,904,707 58

Recapitulation.

For first two years	$88,508,755 80
For first three years	135,435,751 04
For first four years	184,239,826 08
For first five years	234,966,064 12

NOTE.—In the 5th year (July 1, 1886), the $100,000,000 5-10 bonds provided for in the House bill will be redeemable.

There is another matter here which I do not wish to omit. The House has reduced the expenses of issuing the bonds to ¼ of 1 per cent. I know that is founded upon the fact that with the 4 per cents we reduced the expenses to a fraction over a quarter of one per cent.

Senator VOORHEES. You speak of the expenses of sale?

Secretary SHERMAN. The entire expenses of sale. I have got some figures here. The fact is that no government in the world, I think, has ever sold its securities at an expense of less than 1 per cent. until in this country, and we have done it by adopting the popular system. The French, you know, paid a great deal in various ways to the Bank of France, and England has always paid high rates, as has also Germany, but in our country but ½ of 1 per cent. is allowed. During thewar the allowance on all the loans was 1 per cent. The funding act reduced it to ½ of 1 per cent., and very properly, because that was a refunding operation, and not an original borrowing. Here is a table showing the expenses and the nature of the expenses of disposing of the 4 per cent. loan, with the commissions to the syndicate. The amount paid to the syndicate was $386,000. That was in 1877 and the first of 1878. The commissions, however, paid under circulars to every public subscription amount to $1,563,000. Anybody could come in. For the extra force employed there was paid $190,000; extra compensation paid under the act of Congress for clerks who had to work night and day, $10,000; engraving plates, printing, &c., $308,000; transportation, $163,000; incidental expenses, $23,000. The total amount was $2,645,000. The amount allowed by the House would allow no commissions to banks and bankers. Now, I cannot state too strongly the importance of such commissions. With it we can enlist the active assistance of all these financial agencies. Without it we would have them against us or indifferent. The small fraction paid them is insignificant compared to the saving to the government of a prompt and rapid sale of these bonds. This saving is over $1,125,000 a month. No one familiar with this business can doubt but that the aid of banks and bankers will expedite these sales several months. When the sales are under full operation we can then deny commissions, as I did with the 4 per cents; but at the commencement of the loan we must offer them some profit or inducement.

Senator KERNAN. That was in disposing of the 4 per cents.

Secretary SHERMAN. In disposing of the 4 per cents. The amount appropriated was $3,704,000, and we saved $1,058,000, but the whole of that saving was in the sale of the last $300,000,000, when we paid no commission at all; the sales got to running so very well.

Senator FERRY. Have you a percentage of cost?

Secretary SHERMAN. No; but I can give it. It was from one-eighth to one-fourth.

Senator FERRY. There is a prejudice in the public mind in regard to the syndicates, that they have been very expensive, and it might be well to have those figures.

Secretary SHERMAN. The syndicate did not get one-seventh of the entire expense.

Senator WALLACE. The commissions paid to the syndicate amounted to $386,000.

Secretary SHERMAN. I say to you that you cannot start this loan on ¼ of 1 per cent. You have got to follow the usual methods by allowing some commissions on sales.

Senator VOORHEES. How much is provided by the bill?

Senator ALLISON. The bill provides for ¼ of 1 per cent.

The CHAIRMAN. You paid no commission on the last $300,000,000?

Secretary SHERMAN. No; simply because it was selling so fast. On that last loan we gave no commission to anybody. The loan was selling fast enough without.

Senator KERNAN. Is this commission anything except to make the discount when they take a certain amount?

Secretary SHERMAN. That is all. We say to the world, " If you come here and take $10,000 of this loan, we will give you a discount of ⅛ of 1 per cent. If you take $1,000,000, we will give you a discount of ¼ of 1 per cent., and so on.

Senator KERNAN. And towards the last they came so freely that they took them without any discount ?

Secretary SHERMAN. On the two last circulars issued under those loans we did not give anything at all. Indeed we raised the rates. We charged them a premium.

The CHAIRMAN. But the average was about three-eighths of one per cent.

Secretary SHERMAN. Yes; but to commence, we must have a half, for the reason that you cannot purchase paper and make orders for engraving and printing for less, but then towards the end we might save.

Senator KERNAN. You would still expect to get through on a quarter of 1 per cent., but you want to begin on one-half?

Secretary SHERMAN. We got through on between one quarter and three-eighths. The transportation is a very. large item. This is the statement:

Statement showing the expenses of issuing the 4 per cent. consols of 1907.

Commissions paid to the syndicate	$386,369 68
Commissions paid under the circulars	1,563,523 28
Extra force employed	190,633 82
Extra compensation paid	9,968 55
Engraving plates and printing bonds and certificates	308,465 38
Transportation by express, messengers, &c	163,381 29
Incidental expenses	23,460 60
Total amount expended	2,645,802 60
Total amount of subscriptions to the 4 % consols of 1907, to date	697,939,550 00
Amount exchanged for 5-20's and 10-40's	2,895,500 00
Amount of refunding certificates sold	40,012,750 00
Total	740,847,800 00
One-half of one per cent. appropriation on the above amount	3,704,239 00
Amount expended from this fund	2,645,802 60
Remaining unexpended	1,058,436 40

TREASURY DEPARTMENT, SECRETARY'S OFFICE, *July* 1, 1880.

In regard to the fifth section of the bill, Mr. Knox is here and can give you his ideas. I think that this section will rather defeat the object in view. There is an amendment here which is of practical importance that has already been suggested by Senator Beck. The bill does not provide the mode and manner of calling in the bonds that are issued. The act of 1870 provides a mode of redeeming the bonds to be issued under it by paying the last bonds issued first. This bill should contain some provision such as Senator Beck suggested, providing a way in which they should be paid and the notice that should be given.

Senator BECK. Look at line 29 of section 1, and see if we cannot do it in a line there by adding " 30 days" instead of 90 days as now provided.

Secretary SHERMAN. That only relates to the 5 per cents that we redeem, not to the bonds that we are issuing.

Senator BECK. Yes; it says that they shall be interest-bearing notes at the rate of 3 per cent. "redeemable at the pleasure of the United

States," &c., and the "bonds and certificates," that is, those to be issued, "shall be, in all other respects, of like character and subject to the same provisions as the bonds authorized to be issued by the act of July 14, 1870, entitled," &c. Then, after line 29 add "except that they shall be paid after notice of 30 days instead of 90 days as hitherto provided."

Secretary SHERMAN. But you must provide also that the last issued should be paid first, and I think you had better put it in the form of a separate section, similar to the law of 1870. I suggest the following provision:

SEC. 5. The payment of any of the bonds or notes hereby authorized after the expiration of the said terms of one and five years, shall be made in amounts to be determined from time to time by the Secretary of the Treasury, at his discretion, the bonds so to be paid to be distinguished and described by the dates and numbers, beginning for each successive payment with the bonds of each class last dated and numbered, of the time of which intended payment or redemption the Secretary of the Treasury shall give public notice, and the interest on the particular bonds so selected at any time to be paid shall cease at the expiration of one month from the date of such notice.

Senator BECK. That covers the whole question.

Senator ALLISON. You find the provision about taking the last bond first to be a good one in practice rather than to select from the whole number by lot?

Secretary SHERMAN. It holds out a gentle inducement to a man to come in first.

Senator ALLISON. Do you think that a wise provision?

Secretary SHERMAN. There is no objection to it. The last man who takes the bond is the first one to be paid off.

Senator FERRY. Why does it induce another to come in first?

Secretary SHERMAN. Because his bonds will run longer. He will feel that his securities cannot be called in until all the others are paid off, and he will be the more eager to come in to take them. That is the theory of the law. I remember why that was put in. It was put in to induce people to take the bonds more promptly.

Senator VOORHEES. Mr. Secretary, I want to get the precise words that you asked to be inserted in lieu of the term "certificate."

Secretary SHERMAN. "Treasury notes."

Senator VOORHEES. "United States Treasury notes"?

Secretary SHERMAN. No; simply "Treasury notes."

Senator BECK. Is section 4, as it now reads, satisfactory, and does it give you the authority you desire?

Secretary SHERMAN. Yes, sir; I think that is all right.

Senator BECK. That would enable you to take the money out of the Treasury in surplus, so as to make this an appropriation by law.

Secretary SHERMAN. We can reimburse it by the sale of the bonds. It will tend to save interest.

Senator FERRY. In that section it is provided that you shall use not exceeding $50,000,000 of gold and silver coin in the Treasury, and then in another part of the section that you may at any time apply the surplus money in the Treasury.

Secretary SHERMAN. That is over and above.

Senator FERRY. It confines you to $50,000,000.

Secretary SHERMAN. I think myself it ought to be confined, because you would not like to leave the Secretary power to strip the Treasury bare of money.

Senator FERRY. But this leaves a discretion at any time to apply the surplus money.

Secretary SHERMAN. The truth is he has the power now, and has exercised it for twenty years.

Senator FERRY. Then what is the point of fixing $50,000,000 ?

Secretary SHERMAN. That is the limit, and I think a very wise limit.

Senator VOORHEES. I do not know that it would affect the operation of the bill, yet it is an awkward mode of expressing it, it seems to me, because in the forepart of the section there is a limit, and immediately afterwards it is followed by no limit.

Senator KERNAN. That is the surplus money. He is to use money that is held there for another purpose to the amount of $50,000,000.

Secretary SHERMAN. He can use $50,000,000 of the resumption fund.

Senator FERRY. The bill does not say that.

Senator BECK. I understand that the Constitution provides that you can take no money out of the Treasury except by virtue of an appropriation made by law.

Secretary SHERMAN. That is true.

Senator BECK. Therefore, this surplus that you have over and above what is necessary for the sinking fund you cannot use unless there is an appropriation authorizing you to do it.

Secretary SHERMAN. No, we cannot use it. This fund is specially set aside by law for the redemption of United States notes, and the Secretary of the Treasury has no more power to diminish that fund than any other fund.

Senator BECK. Then there is a proviso at the close of section 4 :

That the bonds and certificates so purchased or redeemed shall constitute no part of the sinking fund, but shall be canceled.

That means that you shall not swell up your sinking fund by the use of this money beyond what is otherwise provided.

Secretary SHERMAN. That is right.

Senator ALLISON. That is, you reimburse this fund to sell these bonds.

Secretary SHERMAN. In other words, you take that as capital to begin to redeem with.

Senator FERRY. Is not this $50,000,000 applied to the surplus fund that accumulates in the Treasury?

Secretary SHERMAN. No; that is for resumption.

Senator FERRY. But the phraseology does not express it. The language is, "if in his opinion it shall become necessary to use not exceeding $50,000,000 of the standard gold and silver coin in the Treasury."

Secretary SHERMAN. That is set aside as a redemption fund. The standard gold and silver is part of the resumption fund.

Senator FERRY. Do you make discrimination between the moneys of the Treasury ?

Secretary SHERMAN. We do not. The fact is that the gold and silver are kept there for the purpose of redeeming the legal-tender notes upon presentation, as required by law. Here is a statement showing that the surplus revenues of the government from 1866 to 1880 have varied very much :

Statement showing the net receipts, net expenditures, and surplus revenues of the government for each fiscal year from 1866 to 1880 inclusive.

Year ending June 30—	Net receipts.	Net payments.	Surplus.
1866	$558, 032, 620 06	$520, 809, 416 99	$37, 223, 203 07
1867	490, 634, 010 27	357, 542, 675 16	133, 091, 335 11
1868	405, 638, 083 32	377, 340, 284 86	28, 297, 798 46
1869	370, 943, 747 21	322, 865, 277 80	48, 078, 469 41
1870	411, 255, 477 63	309, 653, 560 75	101, 601, 916 88
1871	383, 323, 944 89	292, 177, 188 25	91, 146, 756 64
1872	374, 106, 867 56	277, 517, 962 67	96, 588, 904 89
1873	333, 738, 204 67	290, 345, 245 33	43, 392, 959 34
1874	289, 478, 755 47	287, 133, 873 17	2, 344, 882 30
1875	288, 000, 051 10	274, 623, 392 84	13, 376, 658 26
1876	287, 482, 039 16	258, 459, 797 33	29, 022, 241 83
1877	269, 000, 586 62	238, 660, 008 93	30, 340, 577 69
1878	257, 763, 878 70	236, 964, 326 80	20, 790, 551 90
1879	273, 627, 184 46	266, 947, 883 53	6, 879, 300 93
1880	333, 526, 610 98	267, 642, 957 78	65, 883, 653 20
Total	5, 326, 752, 062 10	4, 578, 683, 852 19	748, 068, 209 91

TREASURY DEPARTMENT, *January* 21, 1881.

Mr. Knox will state the objections to the fifth section. I am inclined to think the House has fallen into a great error. In the first place, if Congress should pass the bill in its present shape, it would practically prohibit the increase of bank notes at times when they are greatly in demand, and it would stop the retirement of such notes at times when they are redundant. There could be no elasticity in the circulation under the provisions of the fifth section of the House bill. Under the provisions of the bill, a bank cannot retire its own notes until it gets possession of them, and that is practically impossible. If you so limit the power to retire circulation, you prevent them from increasing it. I think the opposite course ought to be pursued—that the banks ought to be encouraged to increase their circulation at certain seasons of the year, and it should be easy to retire their circulation at times when it is not needed.

Senator BECK. Is not the practical effect of it that they are retiring at one time and reissuing at another until there are instances such as I see in the report of the Treasurer, where a bank has had out at one time over $800,000 of circulation when the maximum allowed by law was only $450,000; that they have doubled up the circulation under this mode of retiring and made the United States pay each time for the new notes they took out?

Mr. KNOX. I can explain that.

Secretary SHERMAN. Allow Mr. Knox to explain that. The reasons why section 5 ought not to pass, I think Mr. Knox will state much more fully than I can, because it is full of detail. In connection with our refunding operations, I believe it would be a restraint to have any provision of that kind.

Senator WALLACE. It would have the effect to contract the currency?

Secretary SHERMAN. I think it would have the immediate effect to contract the currency, and to prevent its increase.

The committee adjourned until to-morrow.

WEDNESDAY, *January 26, 1881.*

The committee met pursuant to adjournment, there being present, besides members of the committee, JOHN JAY KNOX, Comptroller of the Currency.

The CHAIRMAN. I invite your attention, Mr. Knox, to the bill (H. R. 4592) to facilitate the refunding of the national debt. For my own part I should be very glad to hear you on the subject of the rate of the bonds both as to time and interest, and then as to the question of the cost of refunding, and as to the provision in regard to the banks.

Mr. KNOX. Mr. Chairman, if you will excuse me, I prefer, as I was summoned on section 5, to begin my observations with that, and I suggest that it would be well to read that and also the two sections which it is proposed to repeal.

The CHAIRMAN. You are speaking now of the act of June 20, 1874, section 4.

Mr. KNOX. Yes, sir. Shall I read the section?

The CHAIRMAN. Read what portions of it you think apply to your present reasoning. Section 5 of the bill is the one now under consideration by you.

Mr. KNOX. I propose to speak first of the last part of section 5.

The CHAIRMAN. The 5th section of this bill is—

SEC. 5. From and after the first day of May, eighteen hundred and eighty-one, the three per centum bonds authorized by the first section of this act shall be the only bonds receivable as security for national-bank circulation, or as security for the safe-keeping and prompt payment of the public money deposited with such banks; but when any such bonds deposited for the purposes aforesaid shall be designated for purchase or redemption by the Secretary of the Treasury, the banking association depositing the same shall have the right to substitute other issues of the bonds of the United States in lieu thereof: *Provided,* That no bond upon which interest has ceased shall be accepted or shall be continued on deposit as security for circulation or for the safe-keeping of the public money; and in case bonds so deposited shall not be withdrawn, as provided by law, within thirty days after interest has ceased thereon, the banking association depositing the same shall be subject to the liabilities and proceedings on the part of the Comptroller provided for in section fifty-two hundred and thirty-four of the Revised Statutes of the United States : *And provided further,* That section four of the act of June twentieth, eighteen hundred and seventy-four, entitled "An act fixing the amount of United States notes, providing for a redistribution of the national-bank currency, and for other purposes," be, and the same is hereby, repealed; and sections fifty-one hundred and fifty-nine and fifty-one hundred and sixty of the Revised Statutes of the United States be, and the same are hereby re-enacted."

Mr. KNOX. Section 4 of the act of June 20, 1874, which it is proposed to repeal, is—

SEC. 4. That any association organized under this act, or any of the acts of which this is an amendment, desiring to withdraw its circulating notes, in whole or in part, may, upon the deposit of lawful money with the Treasurer of the United States in sums of not less than nine thousand dollars, take up the bonds which said association has on deposit with the Treasurer for the security of such circulating notes; which bonds shall be assigned to the bank in the manner specified in the nineteenth section of the national-bank act; and the outstanding notes of said association, to an amount equal to the legal-tender notes deposited, shall be redeemed at the Treasury of the United States, and destroyed as now provided by law : *Provided,* That the amount of the bonds on deposit for circulation shall not be reduced below fifty thousand dollars.

Senator ALLISON. Now please read the sections to be revived.

Mr. KNOX. Section 5159 of the Revised Statutes is as follows:

SEC. 5159. Every association, after having complied with the provisions of this Title, preliminary to the commencement of the banking business, and before it shall be authorized to commence banking business under this Title, shall transfer and deliver to the Treasurer of the United States any United States registered bonds, bearing interest, to an amount not less than thirty thousand dollars and not less than one-third of the capital stock paid in. Such bonds shall be received by the Treasurer upon deposit, and shall be by him safely kept in his office, until they shall be otherwise disposed of, in pursuance of the provisions of this Title.

Section 5160 reads:

SEC. 5160. The deposit of bonds made by each association shall be increased as its capital may be made up or increased, so that every association shall at all times have on deposit with the Treasurer registered United States bonds to the amount of at least one-third of its capital stock actually paid in. And any association that may desire to reduce its capital or to close up its business and dissolve its organization, may take up its bonds upon returning to the Comptroller its circulating notes in the proportion hereinafter required, or may take up any excess of bonds beyond one-third of its capital stock, and upon which no circulating notes have been delivered.

Senator ALLISON. Those sections are proposed to be re-enacted.

Senator FERRY. Before you go on, Mr. Knox, let me ask you if the provision as to "one-third of the capital stock" is not in conflict with the requirement that $50,000 is the minimum that banks can deposit before organizing?

Senator BECK. The National Bank of Missouri failed for two and a half millions, and only had $50,000 of bonds on deposit, I believe, when it ought to have had over $800,000.

Mr. KNOX. If the committee please, I will first refer to the act of June 20, 1874, and the retirement and issue of circulating notes, in a very brief manner.

Early in the year 1874 two bills were introduced in Congress, one in the House on January 27, 1874, which passed on June 20 of the same year, and the other in the Senate on March 23, 1874. This last bill was a substitute for a bill previously introduced and passed by both Houses, but was vetoed by the President and failed to become a law. These bills at the outset contained similar provisions, and both received the attention of the country and elicited exhaustive discussion in both houses. One principal object of each was to bring about an equalization of the currency. It was said that the New England States had an excess of $70,000,000 of national bank notes, and that the Eastern and Middle States together had three fourths of all the circulation of the national banks; that Massachusetts had $38,000,000 in excess of its true proportions; that Rhode Island had $10,000,000 in excess; Connecticut, $11,000,000; New York, $2,500,000; Pennsylvania, $3,500,000; that Virginia was deficient, $4,000,000; Georgia, $4,500,000; Missouri, $9,000,000; and that the whole South taken together was deficient $51,000,000. It was said that while the average ratio per capita was $9.18, Rhode Island had $61 per capita; Massachusetts had $41; and Connecticut, $33; while 14 other States combined had but $5.78. The Eastern States, it was claimed, had $31.68 per capita; the Middle States, $12.82; the Southern States, $2.91; the Western States, $7,09; and the Pacific States but $1.82. We did not at that time take sufficiently into consideration the fact, which has since become apparent, that bills of exchange, checks, deposits, the clearing house, the telegraph, and the cable, have diminished the necessity for an equal distribution of circulating notes throughout the country; that the transactions of the clearing-house are a better test of the volume of business of any section of the country than is the amount of paper money which it contains; and that the mere issue of circulating notes cannot of itself convert poverty into plenty.

Reference is made to these bills for the purpose of reminding the committee of the prolonged consideration which was given to section 4 of the act of June 20, 1874, which it is now proposed to repeal. The Senate bill, known as the resumption act, was introduced on December

21, 1874, and became a law on January 14, 1875, about seven months after the act of June 20, 1874. The last named act—

1st. Reduces the reserve of the national banks by repealing the section requiring a reserve to be kept on circulation.

2d. It requires national-banks notes to be redeemed at the Treasury in Washington, at the expense of the bank.

3d. It provides for the withdrawal of bonds, and the reduction of national-bank circulation at the pleasure of the banks, upon their depositing the required amount of lawful money.

4th. It fixed the maximum amount of legal tender notes at $382,000,000.

5th. It provided for the redistribution of national bank notes authorized by the act of July 12, 1880, by the withdrawal of $55,000,000 of such notes from the States having an excess of their proportion, and its issue to those States having less than their proportion, under an apportionment made on the basis of population and wealth, as shown by the returns of the census of 1870.

This act gave the banks such facilities for reducing their capital and retiring their circulating notes that it was soon found that there was no necessity for withdrawing circulation from one portion of the country in order to supply the demands of other portions.

Section 4 of the act, which it is now proposed to repeal, provides that any bank may reduce its circulation by depositing legal tender notes. During the first year and a half after its passage to November 1, 1875, $15,000,000 of additional circulation was issued, and $20,000,000 retired and destroyed without reissue, and from that date to the present time a greater amount of circulation has been retired under the operation of the act than has been issued; so that the amount originally authorized, $354,000,000, not including the issues of the national gold banks (which is now only $1,135,260), has never been called for, and the amount now outstanding is more than $10,000,000 less than $354,000,000.

This table shows the amount of national-bank currency issued and retired since the passage of the act of June 20, 1874, to January 1, 1881:

	Issued.	Retired.		Total.
		Act of June 20, 1874.	Liquidating.	
From June 20, 1874, to November 1, 1875	$15,721,175	$12,729,814	$4,607,723	$17,337,537
For year ending November 1, 1876	7,093,680	24,392,255	3,114,726	27,506,981
For year ending November 1, 1877	16,306,030	15,578,847	2,686,484	18,265,331
For year ending November 1, 1878	16,291,685	8,301,692	2,684,424	10,986,116
For year ending November 1, 1879	22,933,490	5,258,850	1,781,547	7,040,397
For year ending November 1, 1880	13,402,215	4,873,890	1,319,163	6,193,053
For November and December, 1880	1,607,150	769,843	225,046	994,889
Surrendered between same dates				11,975,565
Totals	93,355,425	71,905,191	16,419,113	100,299,869

Previous to the passage of this act, a national bank desiring to reduce its capital was obliged to pay a premium for its own notes and send them in for destruction before it could accomplish such reduction; and, if sections 5159 and 5160 R. S. should again become the law, no bank in the country whose capital should become impaired could continue its business unless it should make an assessment upon its shareholders for the purpose of restoring such capital. Such a bank may now reduce its capital under the restrictions of the act and retire its circulation, and continue as a legally organized bank.

It is not uncommon for a national bank with small capital to impair that capital to some extent through injudicious loans. The amount of this impairment, if small, can ordinarily be restored by reducing the circulation of the bank and disposing of its bonds, thus utilizing the premium.

The act worked so well that about six months thereafter the resumption act was passed, which authorized free banking. These two acts perfected the legislation in reference to the issue and retirement of bank notes. I mean by this that under the operation of these laws the banks could, all of them, not only reduce their capital at pleasure, but could also reduce and increase their circulation whenever the business of the country seemed to them to make that course desirable. Everybody was satisfied. The banks in the East and the West, the North and the South, could have all the circulation they wished by simply asking for it and conforming to the laws, and the banks having more than was profitable to them could as readily retire it.

The banks promptly deposited the $15,000,000 of lawful money required by the act, and nearly that amount has been continually in the possession of the Treasury. They at first objected to the expense of redemption, which was onerous, but now all have become accustomed to this restriction. The banks pay the expenses of a large force of employés in the Redemption Division of the Treasurer's Office, and the cost of transportation of their notes. In 1876 this expense amounted to the large sum of $365,193.31; in 1877 to $357,066.10; in 1878 to $317,942.48; and in 1879 to $240,949.95.* During the past year the expenses have been less, and the amount redeemed also much less.

The average expense has been about one-ninth of one per cent. upon the circulation, taking these years all together. During the last year it has been considerably less, for the reason that the people of the country prefer paper money to gold coin.

The chief return received by the banks for this large assessment is the right to retire their circulation and take up their bonds, and the corresponding right to redeposit and receive additional circulation whenever they may desire to do so.

Section 5 of the "funding act of 1881" deranges the whole machinery of free banking. It not only prevents the banks from increasing and reducing their circulation at pleasure, but provides in effect, by the re-enactment of sections 5159 and 5160 of the Revised Statutes, for a permanent deposit of bonds, amounting to one-third of the capital of each bank. It also virtually provides that if a bank has too much circulation it shall keep it; if it has too little it shall not increase it unless it shall deposit bonds, which are almost certain to be worth less than par. It subjects the banks to an almost certain loss, and requires them to continue to submit to the loss when they might at times retrieve or diminish it by depositing lawful money in the Treasury and again coming into possession of their own bonds if the market price should be sufficient to justify a sale.

I have tables here, taken from my last annual report, and they are important for a proper understanding of this subject.

On November 1, 1880, according to the most reliable estimates, we had $454,012,030 of gold coin in the country. We also had $690,515,123 of paper money in circulation, consisting of national-bank notes $343,-834,107, and of greenbacks $346,681,016. At that time $200,000,000

---

* Finance Report for 1879, pp. 353–4.

of this $454,000,000 of gold was outside of the banks and the Treasury I include in this statement savings banks, State banks, trust companies, and everything but private bankers.

Senator FERRY. Outside of all these?

Mr. KNOX. What I mean is that there was $200,000,000 of this $454,-000,000 in the hands of the people, and $254,000,000 in the hands of the banks and the government. When I say outside of the banks and the Treasury, I mean it was either in circulation or hoarded.

Senator BECK. Do you mean exclusive of private bankers?

Mr. KNOX. No; I do not include private bankers, because I have no means of getting at the facts as to them.

Senator BECK. Do you include only national banks?

Mr. KNOX. National banks, State banks, savings banks, and trust companies. That is the fact about gold. We had $690,000,000 of paper money in the country, and of that amount $534,000,000 outside of the Treasury and the banks, which fact shows the preference of the people of this country for paper money over coin, and also illustrates the point that I have made as to the difficulty which the banks would experience in procuring their own notes for return to the Treasury, for the purpose of taking up their bonds. A few years ago nearly all the money that the banks held was paper money, for at times all the national banks in the country combined did not have over $9,000,000 in gold coin. Their reserves were then larger than they now are; the law required them to be larger; and nearly all those reserves were in paper money, and largely composed of bank notes; so that it was comparatively easy at that time to return their own notes. It was really difficult then, but it was comparatively easy in comparison with the present time.

This table shows the amount of coin and currency in the country on January 1 and November 1, 1879, and on November 1 of the present year; the amounts of silver and gold coin, which include the bullion in the Treasury, being the estimates of the Director of the Mint:

	January 1, 1879.	November 1, 1879.	November 1, 1880.
Legal-tender notes	$346,681,016	$346,681,016	$346,681,016
National-bank notes	323,791,674	337,181,418	343,834,107
Gold coin	278,310,126	355,681,532	454,012,030
Silver coin	106,573,803	126,009,537	158,271,327
Total	1,055,356,619	1,165,553,503	1,302,798,430

And this table gives the amount of currency and coin in the Treasury at the same dates, and the amount in the national banks, on the dates of their returns nearest thereto—namely, January 1 and October 2, 1879, and October 1, 1880, respectively. The amount given for the State banks and trust companies and the savings banks is at the nearest comparative dates of their official reports. The banks in the State of California report their coin and currency in the aggregate, and in this table the coin is estimated to be three-fourths of the total amount and the currency one-fourth.

	January 1, 1879.	November 1, 1879.	November 1, 1880.
Gold—In the Treasury, less certificates	$112, 703, 342	$156, 907, 986	$133, 679, 349
In national banks	35, 039, 201	37, 187, 238	102, 851, 032
In State banks	10, 937, 812	12, 171, 292	17, 102, 130
Total gold	158, 680, 355	206, 266, 516	253, 632, 511
Silver—In the Treasury, standard silver dollars	17, 249, 740	32, 115, 073	47, 156, 588
In the Treasury, bullion	9, 121, 417	3, 824. 931	6, 185, 000
In the Treasury, fractional coin	6, 048, 194	17, 854, 327	24. 635, 561
In national banks, including certificates	6, 460, 557	4, 986, 492	6, 495, 477
Total silver	38, 879, 908	58, 780, 823	84, 472, 626
Currency—In the Treasury	77, 615, 655	41, 906, 376	26, 846, 826
In national banks	126, 491, 720	118, 546, 369	86, 439, 925
In State banks	25, 944, 485	25, 555, 280	25, 828, 794
In savings banks	14, 513, 779	15, 880, 921	17, 072, 680
Total currency	244, 565, 639	201, 888, 946	16, 188, 225
Grand totals	422, 125, 902	460, 936, 285	494, 293, 362

The silver certificates, amounting in all to $19,780,241 on November 1, 1880, of which $1,165,120 were held by the national banks, are not included in the above exhibit.

If from the amount of coin and currency in the country, as given in the first table, the amount in the Treasury and the banks be deducted, the remainder will give the amount of each kind then in the hands of the people outside of these depositories, as follows:

	January 1, 1879.	November 1, 1879.	November 1, 1880.
Gold	$119, 629, 771	$149, 415, 016	$200, 379, 519
Silver	67, 693, 895	67, 228, 714	73, 798, 701
Currency	425, 907, 051	481, 973, 488	534, 326, 898
Totals	613, 230, 717	698, 617, 218	808, 505, 118

Senator ALLISON. Before you pass from the question of gold coin, Mr. Knox, I should like to ask you a question. You say that 200 millions of this gold is outside of the banks and the Treasury. Do you include bullion in that?

Mr. KNOX. No; some of the gold in possession of the government in the mints and assay office of New York is bullion.

Senator ALLISON. You must have some general idea as to the different hoards, or places where that money is held.

Mr. KNOX. I know what the national banks have.

Senator ALLISON. I speak of the 200 millions outside of the banks and the Treasury. Where, in your judgment, is that to be found?

Mr. KNOX. It is pretty well scattered. Nearly all of the gold which is in New York City, for instance, is either in the treasurer's office, the assay office, or in the national and State banks There may be, of course, a few individuals who hold some, but the people who live in the cities do not generally hoard coin to any great extent.

Senator ALLISON. Your idea, then, is that this 200 millions of gold is pretty well scattered over the country?

Mr. KNOX. Yes.

Senator FERRY. Held by individuals, whether in banks or elsewhere?

Mr. KNOX. Yes.

Senator WALLACE. The old tendency to hoard among the rural population has returned?

Mr. KNOX. I think so.

Senator MORRILL. Do many of the banks hold less than one-third of their stock in bonds now?

Mr. KNOX. I have a table on this subject, which I prepared immediately after the passage of this bill. I have a list which gives by States and principal cities the banks which hold less than one-third of their capital stock in bonds deposited as security for circulation. Under the operation of this bill, if it should become a law, these banks would be required immediately to put in this additional amount of bonds. The banks in the city of New York, as you probably know, do not, as a rule, care much whether they have circulation or not; and in point of fact there are three banks in that city that have never taken out a dollar of circulation, and a fourth one which some time ago surrendered what circulation it then had. At the time of their organization, however, the three banks first named deposited six per cent. bonds to the amount of one-third their capital, as the law required, but they did not ask for any circulation. I believe all of them have since then reduced their bonds on deposit to $50,000. One of them is the Chemical, another is the Fulton, and the third is the City National Bank. The bank which has retired its circulation is the Union National.

This is the table to which I have just referred:

National banks, by States and principal cities, which have less than one-third of their capital in bonds deposited as security for circulation.

State.	Amount of capital.	Amount of bonds.	Amount of bonds required to equal one-third of capital.
MASSACHUSETTS.			
3 banks in the State..........................	$2,400,000	$450,000	$349,999
CONNECTICUT.			
3 banks in the State..........................	2,182,800	414,000	313,599
NEW YORK.			
State .... 3 banks....................	600,000	156,500	43,408
New York City. 18 banks...................	31,300,000	4,584,000	5,849,327
Total..... 21 banks in the State	31,900,000	4,740,500	5,892,825
PENNSYLVANIA.			
State .... 1 bank....................	200,000	50,000	16,666
Philadelphia.... 1 bank....................	600,000	150,000	50,000
Pittsburgh ..... 1 bank....................	200,000	50,000	16,666
Total..... 3 banks in the State	1,000,000	250,000	83,332
MARYLAND.			
Baltimore ...... 1 bank in the State	1,000,000	100,000	233,333
NORTH CAROLINA.			
1 bank in the State..........................	250,000	50,000	33,333
SOUTH CAROLINA.			
2 banks in the State..........................	950,000	150,000	166,666
LOUISIANA.			
New Orleans.... 2 banks in the State	725,000	100,000	141,666

National banks, by States and principal cities, &c.—Continued.

State.	Amount of capital.	Amount of bonds.	Amount of bonds required to equal one-third of capital.
INDIANA.			
3 banks in the State	$900,000	$150,000	$150,000
ILLINOIS.			
State............ 1 bank	250,000	75,000	8,332
Chicago .... 6 banks	3,250,000	350,000	733,330
Total ..... 7 banks in the State	3,500,000	425,000	741,663
MICHIGAN.			
3 banks in the State	600,000	150,000	116,665
WISCONSIN.			
1 bank in the State	250,000	50,000	33,333
MINNESOTA.			
3 banks in the State	2,100,000	350,000	349,999
MISSOURI.			
Saint Louis..... 3 banks in the State	1,450,000	100,000	323,332
Total number of banks in United States, 56 ...			8,929,745

Senator MORRILL. If the five and six per cent. bonds should all be retired, would that compel the banks to purchase any of the new bonds at three per cent?

Mr. KNOX. It would, under the fifth section, as it now stands.

Senator FERRY. What burden would it be upon national banks to compel them to deposit, up to one-third of their capital in bonds, more than the present banking law requires.

Mr. KNOX. The total amount in the table here is nearly $9,000,000.

Senator FERRY. It would require that much more on the present capital of the national banks?

Mr. KNOX. Yes. In this statement I give the aggregates by States and principal cities. The amount to be deposited by eighteen banks in New York City would be $5,849,327. So you will see that more than one-half—in fact, nearly two-thirds of the amount would have to be deposited by banks in New York City alone.

Senator MORRILL. What is the amount that is held by banks now of the 4 and 4½ per cents.?

Mr. KNOX. The amount is just about $150,000,000.

Senator ALLISON. What of bonds that are to be redeemed?

Mr. KNOX. I have a table that gives complete information as to the bonds held by national banks to secure circulation.

Senator FERRY. Before you pass to that, is it not a greater security to the people of the country to have a basis of one-third rather than an absolute amount of $50,000,000? Does it not increase the security?

Mr. KNOX. In a very large bank the margin on the bonds would, perhaps, amount to something; but taking the banks collectively, it would probably be very little. I do not think the object of the law in requiring a deposit of bonds was to secure the depositors of the banks, and it was certainly not its purpose to secure their shareholders.

Senator FERRY. Then that feature of the bill is not very objectionable. It does not matter much either way whether it be $50,000 deposit as the minimum, or one-third of the capital?

Mr. KNOX. Suppose the case of a bank with $300,000 capital. This bill requires them to keep $100,000 of bonds on deposit. If the bonds were at par in the market there would in this case be a margin of 10 per cent., $10,000 in all, but only $5,000 in excess of the present law.

Senator FERRY. Under the present law they might still keep up their organization with but $50,000, so that $100,000 would be double security to the people.

Mr. KNOX. At present there would be an excess of $5,000 over the circulation secured, while under the proposed bill there would be an excess of $10,000.

Senator BECK. I want to read you part of a communication I hold in my hand in this very connection, and ask you about it. This is a communication favoring a return to the old law of 1864, the section that the House has inserted, and it makes this statement:

It is a provision in the interest of stockholders of national banks, who will, if it is re-enacted, upon failure of their bank, find assets to the extent of at least one-third of its capital, which will reduce their individual liability to assessment to that extent. For instance, the National Bank of the State of Missouri failed in 1877; nominal capital, $2,500,000; all there was left, however, at date of failure was $50,000 in bonds on deposit in the office. Had the provision in question been in force, there would have been over $800,000 here.

Why ought not the bank, for the benefit of its stockholders and everybody else, to comply with the law as to one-third, and keep it there? That is what I want you to explain. This is the statement of the Treasurer of the United States, who insists on the re-enactment of this law for the security of the people.

Mr. KNOX. The directors of a bank are the agents of the shareholders, and are elected by them to manage the affairs of the bank. If the shareholders of the National Bank of the State of Missouri had been sufficiently careful in the selection of the directors of the bank, its failure would not have occurred, whether it had a large or a small amount of bonds on deposit.

Senator BECK. Then it is your idea that the Government of the United States has no sort of interest in protecting bank depositors, stockholders, or anybody else, except to enable the bank to make all the money it likes.

Mr. KNOX. I do not say that.

Senator BECK. Tell us what you do say.

Mr. KNOX. I said that the stockholders themselves should elect proper officers and directors of the bank to manage their business. The National Bank of the State of Missouri had the largest capital of any bank outside of the city of New York. The national-bank act does not propose to protect shareholders of banks. It simply provides security for circulation, and by its reserves provides for a correct system of banking, which is incidentally a protection to its creditors. If the National Bank of the State of Missouri had invested one-third of its capital, $800,000, in bonds, the margin upon the bonds, after providing for the circulating notes issued, would have been $80,000, which is but 4½ per cent. upon the amount of claims proved, and but 3 per cent. upon the capital; so that it is plain that this feature of the law would afford but very slight benefit either to the creditors or the stockholders. The capital stock of that bank was impaired, and the $80,000 margin might have been of great service in saving the bank, but under the proposed amendment it could not possibly have availed itself of this margin.

About one-half of the banks have a capital of $150,000 or less. The margin on bonds—equal to one-third of the capital of such bank—would be but $5,000. The banks in the aggregate have always held more than one-third of their capital in United States bonds, and there are but few banks which hold less.

Thus the fifth section of the new law will not affect one-half of the banks. As I have already said, the new law will increase the amount of bonds required to be held by a bank having a capital of $300,000 by $50,000. Many of the large banks do not desire circulation, and cannot afford to lock up their capital in the Treasury when it will bear interest at so low a rate as $3\frac{1}{2}$ or 4 per cent.

Senator BECK. Do you regard, therefore, the condition in which the National Bank of the State of Missouri was found at the time of its failure, with only $50,000 in bonds on deposit here, when one-third would have been over $800,000, as a provision of law that we ought to maintain instead of going back to the system that required them to hold one-third of their capital in bonds?

Mr. KNOX. Well, in the case of the National Bank of the State of Missouri we shall pay fully the depositors of the bank. Ninety-five per cent. has been paid already.

Senator BECK. I am speaking of the system that permits that to be done.

Mr. KNOX. I think the system of depositing bonds was intended exclusively for the security of the circulating notes.

Senator BECK. I thought the bonds of the United States were held for all the notes in circulation, leaving 10 per cent. margin.

The CHAIRMAN. The notes of that bank were fully protected, of course?

Mr. KNOX. Certainly that was the theory of the law, that the bonds were deposited as security for the circulation.

Senator BECK. The banks in the big cities have to hold 25 per cent. and in others 15 per cent. of their capital, also to give security.

Senator FERRY. The question comes here, Mr. Beck, whether you can require of national banks any more deposited than what the government issues in circulation—90 per cent. upon the 100—whether the government can require additional security for the capital or the deposits rather than simply for the circulation, which is now the case. That is the whole question involved.

The CHAIRMAN. There are two things the government does. It requires not simply the deposit of bonds to protect the circulating notes, but the furnishing of a reserve also, which varies from 15 to 25 per cent. Beyond that there is no compulsory security of the bank against the improvidence of the stockholders.

Senator ALLISON. Except the double liability of the stockholders themselves.

The CHAIRMAN. Of course, that is fixed in the law; but the government does not interfere with the improvidence of banking business by a board of directors, who are chosen themselves by the voluntary action of the stockholders.

Senator MORRILL. I ask the Comptroller how many bonds do the banks hold bearing interest above $4\frac{1}{2}$ per cent.?

Mr. KNOX. About 50 millions of 6's of 1880 and 1881, and of funded 5's of 1881, 160 millions; $530,000 of the 6's are now due, and there are $49,357,850 of the 6's which mature June 30, 1881. There are also $160,142,850 of the 5 per cent. bonds that mature May 1, 1881.

Senator MORRILL. Making about $210,000,000?

Mr. KNOX. Yes, sir. Now, as to the other classes of bonds, we have of the 4's $109,039,300; of the 4½'s, $36,460,550; and of the Pacifics, $3,916,000, making, as you see, in the aggregate, about $150,000,000, which is one-third of the capital of the banks. So that, taking the banks, to-day, in the aggregate, they hold one-third of their capital in bonds, outside of those bonds which have matured.

This table exhibits the classes and amounts of United States bonds held on this day to secure the redemption of the circulating notes of national banks:

10-40s—5%, act March 3, 1864	$445,700
Sixes of '80—6%, act February 8, 1861	530,000
Sixes of '81—6%, redeemable June 30, 1881	49,357,850
Funded 81s—5%, redeemable May 1, 1881	160,142,850
Pacific Railroad—6%	3,916,000
Funded '91s—4½%	36,460,550
Funded 1907s—4%	109,039,300
Total	$359,892,250

Senator MORRILL. Can you tell what the profit is to the banks, now, on their circulation, and what it would be on 3 per cent. and 3½ per cent. bonds?

On 4 per cent. bonds, at 12 per cent. premium, where interest is 5 per cent., the profit would be 1.69 per cent.; where interest is 6 per cent., it would be about 1.42; with interest at 7 per cent., 1.16; with interest at 8 per cent., .89; where interest is 9 per cent., .63; where interest is 10 per cent., .36, and where interest is 11 per cent., .10.

On 3½ per cent. bonds at par, the profit, where interest is 5 per cent., would be 1.79; where interst is 6 per cent., 1.64; where interest is 7 per cent., 1.49; where interest is 8 per cent., 1.35; where interest is 9 per cent., 1.21; where interest is 10 per cent., 1.06; where interest is 11 per cent., .91.

On 3 per cent. bonds at par, the profit would be, where interest is 5 per cent., 1.29; where interest is 6 per cent., 1.14; where interest is 7 per cent., 1; where interest is 8 per cent., .85; where interest is 9 per cent., .71; where interest is 10 per cent., .56; where interest is 11 per cent., .41. This table gives the information:

Profits on circulation on deposit of bonds bearing interest at 4 per cent., 3½ per cent., and 3 per cent., the circulation received being equal to 90 per cent. of the par value of bonds, when the rates for bank loans are as specified.

	5 per cent.	6 per cent.	7 per cent.	8 per cent.	9 per cent.	10 per cent.	11 per cent.
4 per cent. bonds at 12 per cent. premium...	1.69	1.42	1.16	.89	.63	.36	.10
3½ per cent. bonds at par	1.79	1.64	1.49	1.35	1.21	1.06	.91
3 per cent. bonds at par	1.29	1.14	1.00	.85	.71	.56	.41

Senator MORRILL. In all the [Atlantic cities, throughout the past year, the commercial rate of interest has been less than 6 per cent., has it not?

Mr. KNOX. Yes. The Secretary put in yesterday a paragraph, taken from my last report, which gives the rate of interest in New York City.

Here is the rate on the 25th of January, instant, taken from the New York Daily Bulletin :

CURRENCY PAPER.

	Sixty days.	Four months.
Double-named :		
First class	4½ @ 5	5 @ 5¼
Good	5 @ 6	5½ @ 6
Single-named :		
First class	5 @ 6	5 @ 6
Good	7 @ 8	7 @ 8
Not so well known	9 @ 10	9 @ 10

This is the table which I handed to the Secretary yesterday.

The average rate of interest in New York City for each of the fiscal years from 1874 to 1880, as ascertained from data derived from the Journal of Commerce and the Commercial and Financial Chronicle, was as follows :

1874, call loans, 3.8 per cent. ; commercial paper, 6.4 per cent.
1875, call loans, 3.0 per cent. ; commercial paper, 5.6 per cent.
1876, call loans, 3.3 per cent. ; commercial paper, 5.3 per cent.
1877, call loans, 3.0 per cent. ; commercial paper, 5.2 per cent.
1878, call loans, 4.4 per cent. ; commercial paper, 5.1 per cent.
1879, call loans, 4.4 per cent. ; commercial paper, 4.4 per cent.
1880, call loans, 4.9 per cent. ; commercial paper, 5.3 per cent.
Calendar year 1880, call loans, 3.8 per cent.; commercial paper, 4.7 per cent.

The CHAIRMAN. Please explain why the profit on national-bank circulation is greater where the commercial rate of interest is less.

Mr. KNOX. Suppose you were to organize a bank of say $100,000 capital ; you would buy $100,000 of bonds, for which you would receive $90,000 only in circulating notes. Now you have $10,000 invested in these bonds, for which you do not receive any circulation whatever. That amount is permanently invested capital. If the bonds are 3 per cents, then, when the commercial rate of interest is 10 per cent., there is a loss of 7 per cent. on the $10,000 invested. If the commercial rate of interest is only 6 per cent., as in New England, there is then a loss of only 3 per cent. instead of 7 per cent. on the margin named. Of course, if you buy at a premium, that would occasion a still greater loss.

Senator FERRY. Is this computation of amount of profit based on the whole $100,000 deposited ?

Mr. KNOX. The percentages given are the profits on circulation, issued to the amount of 90 per cent. of the bonds deposited.

Senator FERRY. But do you take into consideration now the whole deposit, and the difference of interest on $10,000 ?

Mr. KNOX. Yes.

Senator BECK. The banks lose on the 10 per cent. margin by the rate of interest being 7 per cent., but they have received $90,000 that they are loaning at 7 per cent., and they are getting that additional interest on the $90,000 while they are losing on the $10,000; and I cannot see where the loss comes in ultimately. When money is worth 7 per cent., are they not getting 7 per cent. on the $90,000 the United States furnishes them ? They deposited $100,000 of bonds, and they have got $90,000 of circulation, and they are loaning that at 7 per cent. Therefore, they are only losing the difference in the interest between the rate on the bonds and the rate of interest on the 10 per cent. margin. Now they are getting a much higher rate of interest on the $90,000 that they received; and does not the whole put together make them a larger profit when interest is higher?

Mr. KNOX. We were talking about the profits of circulation alone.

Senator BECK. But the whole business makes them money.

Mr. KNOX. Here is our system of calculating the profits of circulation: One hundred thousand dollars in United States 4 per cent. bonds will cost a bank, at current rates, at least $112,000. On these bonds, when deposited in the Treasury, the bank receives $90,000 in circulation. The amount which is available to be loaned is reduced from $90,000 to $73,500, first by the payment of the premium of $12,000 on the bonds purchased, and, second, by the 5 per cent. reserve required, viz, $4,500. The bank receives 4 per cent. per annum on its bonds, or $4,000. If it lends its loanable circulation at 6 per cent., it receives $4,410 more. In all, it receives $8,410. From this sum must be deducted the 1 per cent. tax on circulation, amounting to $900, leaving $7,510 of profit to the bank. If the bank's capital of $100,000 had been loaned directly at 6 per cent., it would have realized $6,000, so that the profit from $90,000 of circulation, upon a deposit of United States 4 per cent. bonds at 112, and, when the rate of interest for bank loans is 6 per cent., is $1,510, or about 1½ per cent. on the sum invested. This amount should be reduced still further by the expense of redeeming the circulation. This expense the Treasurer of the United States, in his last report, estimates to have been $37.69 in 1880 for banks with a circulation of $90,000. This amount is too small, as a computation based on the cost of redemptions during the past five years shows. During this period of five years the average cost of the total redemptions of national-bank notes has been $284,975.54, while the average outstanding circulation, including the notes of banks insolvent and in liquidation, and excluding those of gold banks, has been $328,459,161. The percentage has therefore been about nine one-hundredths of 1 per cent., or $81 per year for a bank with $90,000 circulation.

As seen above, the profits on circulation of a bank of this class are $1,510, not deducting the expense of redemptions. Deducting this expense, the profits are $1,429.

The above computation is concisely stated as follows:

Interest on $100,000 U. S. 4 per cent. bonds		$4,000
Circulation issued on above.........$90,000		
Deduct premium............$12,000		
Deduct reserve.............. 4,500		
	16,500	
Leaving loanable circulation..	73,500, 6 per cent. interest on which is..	4,410
Total interest received		8,410
Deduct 1 per cent. tax	$900	
Deduct cost of redemptions	81	
		981
Leaving as net receipts		7,429
$100,000 capital loaned direct at 6 per cent		6,000
Difference in favor of circulation		1,429

Senator MORRILL. Mr. Knox, would you recommend the striking out of this whole fifth section, or only an amendment to it?

Mr. KNOX. I have here a statement prepared by Mr. Elliott. There was one somewhat like it submitted by the Secretary, I believe, showing what the value of 3 per cent. bonds would be in proportion to the 4 per cents at 112.

" A United States *four* per cent. bond, redeemable July 1, 1907, and considered as then payable at 112.85, the *net* price, or price *not* including the interest accrued since the last date of payment, on January 25 of the current year, realizes to the investor interest at the rate of 3.27 per cent. per annum.

" In order to realize the same rate of interest (3.27) to the investor, a *three* per cent. bond to run 5, 10, 30, and 50 years, respectively, to payment, must sell at 98.8, 97.7, 94.9, and 93.4, respectively.

" If a *three* per cent. bond sells at par, net price, a *four* per cent. 26½-year bond, to realize the same rate of interest, should sell at 118.2 *net* price, or price not including accrued interest."

That is the calculation of Mr. Elliott, of the Treasury Department. I asked him to give me the figures.

I have a table of the amount of circulation outstanding, which is interesting in this connection, as showing what amount has been called for by the banks, and the amount not called for; by which it appears that there is about $70,000,000 of circulation to which the national banks now in existence are entitled, and might take if they would ask for it.

Senator ALLISON. That is, they have the bonds on deposit for it.

Mr. KNOX. No; they have not the bonds on deposit, but they have sufficient capital to entitle them to it.

Senator ALLISON. But they do not put in the bonds and take the circulation?

Mr. KNOX. No, sir; they do not put in the bonds, at present prices.

Senator ALLISON. Why not?

Mr. KNOX. Because in the West it is not profitable. I will submit the table now:

Geographical divisions.	Banks having capital not exceeding $500,000.		Banks having capital exceeding $500,000.		Total.	
	Issued.	Uncalled for.	Issued.	Uncalled for.	Issued.	Uncalled for.
New England States	$70,322,430	$7,046,763	$43,014,500	$11,485,238	$122,336,930	$18,532,001
Middle States	82,940,955	9,291,590	29,681,740	21,094,833	112,622,695	30,386,423
Southern States	23,162,985	2,620,845	1,370,000	510,000	24,532,985	3,130,845
Western States	52,284,710	11,620,690	5,707,380	4,552,620	57,992,090	16,173,310
Pacific States and Territories	3,244,700	935,800	640,000	560,000	3,884,700	1,495,800
United States	240,955,780	31,515,688	80,413,620	38,202,691	321,369,400	69,718,379

The CHAIRMAN. Is not the amount uncalled for rather an increase from last year? The amount that the banks could take out last year was not as great as is the amount they may take out now.

Mr. KNOX. I believe not. Senator Morrill asked me in reference to this fifth section, whether I would prefer to strike it out or try to amend it.

Senator KERNAN. Or go for it as it is.

Senator MORRILL. I judge from the Comptroller's criticisms of it, that he thinks it ought all to come out.

Mr. KNOX. I should prefer myself to strike out the section entirely; but if it is to remain, then I would suggest some change in its language. You have, Mr. Chairman, a bill that was introduced the other day, I think, at my request, which provides that all the national banks shall receive circulation at the rate of 90 per cent. on their capital. As the law now stands, a bank of $500,000 capital can receive 90 per cent. upon that capital, while one with $1,000,000 capital receives but 80 per cent., receiving, of course, 90 per cent. on its bonds, as do the other banks.

If it has $2,000,000 of capital, it can receive but 75 per cent.; if its capital is $3,000,000, or over, it receives only 60 per cent. That law was the act of March 3, 1865, when we did not have circulation enough to supply all the banks, the total amount being limited to $300,000,000. Up to March 3, 1865, every bank was entitled to receive circulation equal to the amount of its capital. There is another reason why I would like the amendment suggested. The original section of the Revised Statutes is somewhat obscure, and an amendment like this, for instance, would make it plain:

And any bank depositing bonds shall be entitled to receive circulation to the amount of its capital, at the rate of 90 per cent. upon such bonds.

Senator FERRY. So as to make no discrimination and no limitation. That, you say, was the law prior to 1865?

Mr. KNOX. That was the law prior to 1865. We have a bank at Saint Paul and one at Cincinnati, and banks in other localities, organized within a few years, and each having a capital of a million dollars, and neither of them can have now more than $500,000 circulation. That, however, is on account of another section of the Revised Statutes, section 5176, which provides that no bank organized subsequent to July 12, 1870, shall have a circulation in excess of $500,000.

Senator FERRY. What is the object in scaling the privilege in any respect?

Mr. KNOX. There is no reason now. The only reason then was that there was not sufficient circulation, as I have before stated.

Senator FERRY. Now that it is free to all, there is no object in it; there is no greater security to the people?

Mr. KNOX. None.

Senator BECK. How much circulation did we have in paper on the 1st day of July, 1874, and how much did we have on the 1st day of July, 1880?

Mr. KNOX. I shall have to give it to you for January, 1874. Legal-tender notes, $378,400,000, and bank notes $350,800,000.

Senator BECK. My memorandum is that on the 1st of July, 1874, we had a total of $781,000,000, and on the 1st day of July, 1880, $735,000,000, being, in round numbers, $45,000,000 less now than we had then.

Senator FERRY. And what is it to-day?

Mr. KNOX. On November 1, 1880, we had of legal tenders $346,000,000, and of bank notes $343,000,000.

Senator BECK. What I wanted to get at was this: My table shows that we had $45,000,000 more of paper circulation on the 1st of July, 1874, than we had on the 1st of July, 1880, notwithstanding all the growth of the country and the increase of business. I do not see how we are in any better position to remove the limitation of circulation of the large banks now than we were then.

The CHAIRMAN. You do not say anything of coin.

Senator BECK. No, sir.

Senator ALLISON. But you include in your total, Mr. Beck, $45,000,000 of fractional currency.

Senator BECK. I suppose it is included in both statements.

Senator ALLISON. No; the Comptroller is not including it in his statement.

Senator BECK. These two are as to July 1, 1874, and July 1, 1880.

Senator ALLISON. But that $45,000,000 of fractional currency has been replaced by silver.

Mr. KNOX. Exclusive of fractional currency we had about $690,000,000 of paper money, and we had on the 1st of January, 1874, $729,000,000.

Senator BECK. Then how is it we are so much more able now to issue more paper? You say they were limited because of the want of paper money, and you can now give them all they want, because we have an abundance, when we have less now than we had then, according to that showing.

Senator FERRY. Does not that grow out of the existing taxation, and the lack of profit to the banks, really persuading them to retire their currency and take up their bonds?

Mr. KNOX. The profit on circulation has been growing less. Since that day we have retired legal-tender notes, so as to reduce the amount from $378,000,000 to $346,000,000.

Senator BECK. You have to keep $346,000,000 out; that is the volume of legal tenders.

Mr. KNOX. But that is a reduction since 1874.

Senator ALLISON. There has been a diminution of greenbacks, and the fractional currency has been retired; that accounts for the difference.

Mr. KNOX. Yes, sir.

Senator KERNAN. I do not think the fractional currency is included in the tables of Mr. Beck.

Senator ALLISON. Yes; here [exhibiting] is the table from which he takes it, showing that $48,000,000 of the amount he states was fractional currency in 1874.

Mr. KNOX. In my last report, on page 51, I give the items separately.

Here is the table exhibiting the amount and kinds of outstanding paper currency of the United States and of the national banks, on August 31, 1865, when the public debt reached its maximum, and annually thereafter at the dates named, with the currency price of gold and the gold price of currency at the same dates:

Date.	United States issues.			Notes of national banks including gold notes.	Aggregate.	Currency price of $100 gold.	Gold price of $100 currency.
	Legal tender notes.	Old demand notes.	Fractional currency.				
August 31, 1865...	$432,553,912	$402,965	$26,344,742	$176,213,955	$635,515,574	$144 25	$69 32
January 1, 1866...	425,830,319	392,070	26,000,420	298,588,419	750,820,228	144 50	60 20
January 1, 1867...	380,276,160	221,632	28,732,812	299,846,206	709,076,860	133 00	75 18
January 1, 1868...	356,000,000	159,127	31,597,583	299,747,569	687,504,279	133 25	75 04
January 1, 1869...	356,000,000	128,098	34,215,715	299,629,322	689,973,135	135 00	74 07
January 1, 1870...	356,000,000	113,098	39,762,664	299,904,029	695,779,791	120 00	83 33
January 1, 1871...	356,000,000	101,086	39,995,089	306,307,672	702,403,847	110 75	90 29
January 1, 1872...	357,500,000	92,801	40,767,877	328,465,431	726,826,109	109 50	91 32
January 1, 1873...	358,557,907	84,387	45,722,061	344,582,812	748,947,167	112 00	89 28
January 1, 1874...	378,401,702	79,637	48,544,792	350,848,236	777,874,367	110 25	90 70
January 1, 1875...	382,000,000	72,317	46,390,598	354,128,250	782,591,165	112 50	88 83
January 1, 1876...	371,827,220	69,642	44,147,072	346,479,756	762,523,690	112 75	88 69
January 1, 1877...	366,055,084	65,462	26,348,206	321,595,606	714,064,358	107 00	93 46
January 1, 1878...	349,943,776	63,532	17,764,109	321,672,505	689,443,922	102 87	97 21
January 1, 1879...	346,681,016	62,035	16,109,159	323,791,674	686,642,884	100 00	100 00
January 1, 1880...	346,681,016	61,350	15,674,304	342,387,336	704,804,006	100 00	100 00
January 1, 1881...	346,681,016	60,745	7,147,530	344,355,203	698,244,494	100 00	100 00

The CHAIRMAN. Your attention has been drawn to the currency of the national banks and the United States notes together, which make an aggregate less than was apparently the currency in 1874; but what is the volume to-day of currency, treating gold and silver as currency? The circulation has increased.

Mr. KNOX. Wonderfully. We have now, altogether, 1,302 millions, being an increase of 247 millions since January 1, 1879.

Senator KERNAN. Of coin and currency in the country, generally?

Mr. KNOX. Yes, sir.

Senator FERRY. That includes coin and currency?

Mr. KNOX. Yes.

Senator ALLISON. You do not include in the $690,000,000 of paper the silver certificates?

Mr. KNOX. Not at all.

Senator ALLISON. There is a circulation now of several millions of silver certificates, which are paper money.

Mr. KNOX. Eighteen and a half millions were in circulation on November 1, 1880.

Senator KERNAN. But you include the silver on which they are based?

Mr. KNOX. Yes; the silver coin is included There are eighteen or twenty million of silver certificates in circulation now, that I have not included.

Senator ALLISON. They are paper?

Mr. KNOX. Yes.

Senator WALLACE. But the silver they represent is not included in the aggregate of circulation?

Mr. KNOX. Yes; but not the certificates.

Senator FERRY. Those freely circulate?

Mr. KNOX. They circulate in this city freely.

Senator FERRY. Do they elsewhere?

Mr. KNOX. Not generally.

Senator WALLACE. What is the practical effect of the 5th section, as it stands, on the circulation of the national banks?

Mr. KNOX. The object of the act, as I suppose, is to make a market for the bonds therein provided for. I have not yet been able to prepare a list of the bonds held by each bank separately, but that is now being done, and I shall be able to send it to the committee probably within two or three days. I purpose to ascertain what banks hold the five and six per cents, and whether such banks would still hold one-third of their capital in bonds supposing they should retire these five and six per cents, in conformity with the proposed law. We have seen, from a table which I handed in, that the banks, collectively, are now holding more than one-third of their capital in bonds, but that fifty-four banks are each holding less, the deficiency being a little less than $9,000,000. If this section shall be adopted, these fifty-four banks would then be obliged to do one of two things—either to reduce their capital or to purchase more bonds. The banks can now readily reduce their capital, in anticipation of the adoption of this section; but should they not do this, then the passage of the bill would make a market for $9,000,000 of bonds, and $9,000,000 only. I now estimate the amount which the banks would be obliged to buy, after the 5's and 6's which they hold are paid off, at $50,000,000, in order to conform to the law as to one-third of the capital.

Senator KERNAN. So that in no event would there be a market for more than $60,000,000 for the banks?

Mr. KNOX. As I said before, the banks now hold nearly one-third of their capital in 4's and 4½'s. You will find here and there an instance of a bank that is a little below, and another that is a little above; but in those that are below I think the aggregate deficiency will not be much over $60,000,000.

The CHAIRMAN. Then you say a compulsory market under that section would not be found for more than how many bonds?

Mr. KNOX. It would not probably oblige the banks to buy much over $60,000,000; but, then, it seems to me that legislation of that kind has the appearance of forcing the banks to buy bonds; any one who is urged to do a thing against his judgment hesitates, and perhaps declines altogether.

The CHAIRMAN. May I ask you what do you suppose is the amount of bonds of the United States which the banks are obliged to deposit for safe keeping as collateral security for the public deposits with them?

Mr. KNOX. I have that information.

Senator BECK. The law now allows them to deposit other things as well as bonds, for the safe-keeping of the public money; and this would open a market to the extent that it made these bonds the exclusive deposit.

The CHAIRMAN. What is the amount they are required to deposit?

Senator BECK. They can give a mortgage on property.

Mr. KNOX. I think there are a few banks on the frontier that do not furnish government bonds exclusively as security for deposits; but those are exceptional cases. Such banks have, perhaps, in addition to their bonds, put in some other personal security. I am not certain that there is any such case at present, but there were instances of that kind in the beginning of the system. I think there was one case in Montana, some years ago, where an additional bond was offered as such security by a national bank, and it was taken in addition to the government bonds. It is the intention of the government always to have an amount of security in excess of the government deposits. I think the amount of bonds now held by the Treasurer would cover the deposits.

Senator BECK. But the law allows other securities?

Mr. KNOX. The law does not strictly require that they shall be government bonds.

Senator BECK. Now give us the amount, please, as the chairman asked you.

Mr. KNOX. It was $14,800,000 on the 1st day of October last.

The CHAIRMAN. That was collateral security given to the government when the government makes deposits with the banks. Is that it?

Mr. KNOX. Yes, sir.

Senator BECK. The First National Bank of New York, a year ago, is reported to have had $128,000,000 of government money lying in its vaults. It must have been much larger than that.

, Mr. KNOX. It was large at that time.

Senator ALLISON. That was during the process of refunding.

The CHAIRMAN. To enlighten myself, may I ask you this question: I have heard it stated that as much as $250,000,000 would be deposited with the banks at times, and that there would be requisite under this act an equal amount of three per cent. bonds, if the banks desired to receive the deposits; in other words, there would be a market created for $250,000,000 of the three per cent. bonds, to be employed by the banks as their special security for government deposits. What is your criticism on that statement?

Mr. KNOX. I do not know of any such transaction as that. I have personally nothing to do with the matter of receiving bonds as security for government deposits, nor have I anything to do with government deposits at all.

The CHAIRMAN. What officer of the Treasury could answer?

Mr. KNOX. Mr. Upton, the assistant secretary, can give you the facts about it. You will find that on April 4, 1879, the banks had on deposit in the Treasury 309 millions of United States bonds as security for government deposits, and that on June 14 following they held 257 millions. That was in the midst of the refunding operations, and by reference to page 150 of my last report you will find the amount was reduced to 18 millions on October 2 of that year and to 14 millions on December 12, at which amount it has remained to the present time.

Senator BECK. So that makes what the chairman says, that at times there are very large amounts held.

Mr. KNOX. Yes, sir; during the enormous refunding operations of that year only.

Senator FERRY. You make out that fourteen or fifteen million will be required as security for the government funds deposited with the banks, and that $60,000,000 would be taken by the banks, making in all about $75,000,000. What additional amount of three per cents, including the surplus money in the country, in your opinion, would be taken of the short bonds, under the clause as to one, two, or three years' redeemable notes?

Mr. KNOX. I do not know whether I quite understand you.

Senator FERRY. How many Treasury notes under this clause, calling them Treasury notes instead of certificates, as they should properly be called, would probably be taken by the banks, including the $75,000,000 already mentioned? How much of the surplus money of the banks would they absorb, in your judgment?

Mr. KNOX. I think in regard to these certificates that the banks would not themselves take them at first, but would probably receive them after they should get into circulation. I think the certificates would work something like the compound-interest notes formerly issued by the government. The certificates would probably go into circulation temporarily, and the banks would then take them. Some of them would receive the certificates at par, after interest had accrued, and some of them would perhaps pay a little portion of the interest as it accrued.

Senator KERNAN. Would they loan on them, making short loans to their customers?

Mr. KNOX. Certainly.

Senator FERRY. In other words, can $300,000,000, or, if not, what amount, of these fifty-dollar certificates, as they are named here, be placed, in your judgment, on the terms stated in the bill?

Mr. KNOX. I should think nothing like $300,000,000.

Senator FERRY. What amount do you think? You have already $75,000,000 provided for in the banks.

Mr. KNOX. I do not suppose that the Secretary would undertake to issue the certificates and sell the bonds at the same time. The operations would interfere very much with each other.

Senator FERRY. I want to call your attention in that connection to the requirements of the sinking fund, which can as well be placed in the three per cents as in any other bonds. In five years the sinking fund will require $200,000,000, because your requirement for the coming year is $46,000,000, and last year was $40,000,000.

Mr. KNOX. That all represents bonds.

Senator FERRY. Here you have $75,000,000 that the banks would take; adding $200,000,000 for the sinking fund crowds very closely on the $300,000,000 in this bill.

Senator ALLISON. The banks would not take the $75,000,000 in certificates; they would take bonds.

Mr. KNOX. They would not be likely to subscribe for certificates.

Senator FERRY. Taking into consideration the sinking fund, what, in your judgment, would be the maximum amount of these certificates, as they are called in the bill, that could be placed?

Mr. KNOX. I do not feel like making an estimate. This matter of the certificates and the loans is rather out of my department.

Senator FERRY. Have you no judgment on it?

Mr. KNOX. I should estimate the amount of the certificates at from 100 millions to 150 millions.

Senator MORRILL. And they would not come in until after the negotiation of the bonds?

Mr. KNOX. No, sir.

Senator ALLISON. I was going to ask you for a little information. I should like to know whether the national banks are paying large dividends or small ones, or what they are doing?

Mr. KNOX. I have a table upon that subject. The banks were more prosperous during the last year than for several years previous. Their dividends for that year were about 7 per cent. For the years 1878 and 1879 their dividends were between 6 and 7 per cent.

Senator BECK. Is not that profit both upon their capital and surplus?

Mr. KNOX. No, sir; it is on the capital.

Senator BECK. Independent altogether of the surplus?

Mr. KNOX. Yes, sir. I think the proper ratio should be on the capital and surplus.

Senator BECK. What is the ratio on capital and surplus?

Mr. KNOX. During the first six months of 1880 it was 3.17 per cent., and for the six months ending September 1, 1880, it was 3.18 per cent., in all 6.35 per cent.

Senator BECK. On capital and surplus both?

Mr. KNOX. Yes, sir.

Senator BECK. After paying all the expenses of the banks?

Mr. KNOX. Yes, sir. In 1879 it was 6.7 per cent.; in 1878, 6.21 per cent. In this connection it may be stated that during the first six months of last year there were 269 banks that did not pay any dividends at all.

Senator ALLISON. Paid no dividends?

Mr. KNOX. No dividends at all, and 290 banks in the second six months paid no dividends at all.

Senator FERRY. Owing to losses?

Mr. KNOX. On account of their losses. The law provides that if any bank has met with losses it shall not pay dividends. Its charter is liable to forfeiture at any time for paying a dividend when it has not earned the money. The banks have no right to pay out their capital in dividends. Particular attention is paid to this feature of the system, and close scrutiny is given to the reports of the examiners, and those of the banks themselves, to see that it is not violated.

Senator BECK. Let me understand that. That 6.35 per cent. on capital and surplus is the average, including all those banks that made nothing?

Mr. KNOX. Yes, sir; that is the average of the whole.

Senator BECK. Broken banks and all?

Mr. KNOX. No broken banks.

Senator BECK. Non-dividend-paying banks?

Mr. KNOX. All banks that are in operation.

This is the table showing the capital, surplus, dividends, and total earnings of all the national banks for each half year, from March 1,

1878, to September 1, 1880, together with the ratio of dividends to capital and to capital and surplus, and of earnings to capital and surplus:

Period of six months ending—	No. of banks.	Capital.	Surplus.	Total dividends.	Total net earnings.	RATIOS.		
						Dividends to capital.	Dividends to capital and surplus.	Earnings to capital and surplus.
Mar. 1, 1878	2,074	475,609,751	122,373,561	18,982,390	16,946,696	3.99	3.17	2.83
Sept. 1, 1878	2,047	470,291,896	118,687,134	17,959,223	13,658,893	3.81	3.04	2.91
Mar. 1, 1879	2,043	464,413,996	116,744,135	17,541,054	14,678,660	3.78	3.02	2.53
Sept. 1, 1879	2,045	455,132.056	115,149,351	17,401,867	16,873.200	3.82	3.05	2.96
Mar. 1, 1880	2,046	454,080,090	117,226,501	18,121,273	21,152,784	3.99	3.17	3.70
Sept. 1, 1880	2,072	454,215,002	120,145,649	18,290,200	24,033,250	4.03	3.18	4.18

And this statement shows by geographical divisions the number of national banks, with their capital, which have paid no dividends to their stockholders during the two semi-annual periods of 1880, together with the totals for each semi-annual period in the four preceding years:

Geographical divisions.	Six months ending—				Average for the year.	
	March 1, 1880.		September 1, 1880.			
	No. of banks.	Capital.	No. of banks.	Capital.	No. of banks.	Capital.
New England States	30	$6,965,000	15	$3,025,000	23	$4,995,000
Middle States	68	9,959,000	73	9,138,000	70	9,548,500
Southern States	29	4,129,000	27	3,945,900	28	4,037,450
Western States and Territories	99	9,354,200	118	10,225,250	109	9,789,725
Totals for 1880	226	30,407,200	233	26,334,150	230	28,370,675
Totals for 1879	309	53,843,700	299	44,576,300	304	49,210,000
Totals for 1878	328	48,797,900	357	58,736,950	343	53,767,425
Totals for 1877	245	40,452,000	288	41,166,200	266	40,809,100
Totals for 1876	235	34,290,320	273	44,057,725	254	39,174,022
Average for five years	269	41,558,224	290	42,974,265	279	42,266,244

Senator ALLISON. Have you a table as to the taxes paid by the banks?

Mr. KNOX. Yes. I have a small table on that subject.

Senator ALLISON. I mean a table including State and national taxes?

Mr. KNOX. Yes; the aggregate taxation. I shall have to give you the figures for 1879, because we do not get the returns of State taxation until the year following their payment. The taxes which the banks paid during the year 1879 were over three per cent. upon their capital.

Senator KERNAN. State, national, and local?

Mr. KNOX. Yes, sir. In the Middle and Western States the ratio of taxes was exactly the same, 3.6 per cent. In the New England and Southern States it was the same, 2.7 per cent., but we have a great many exceptions to this. For instance, the New York City banks paid a tax of 5 per cent.; Albany, 5.4 per cent.; Milwaukee, 5.3 per cent.; and Chicago, 5.8 per cent., on account of the heavy local city taxation. This is the table:

Taxation of National Banks.

1878.

Geographical divisions.	Capital.	Amount of taxes.			Ratios to capital.		
		United States.	State.	Total.	United States.	State.	Total.
					Per ct.	Per ct.	Per ct.
New England States	$166,737,594	$1,900,735	$2,503,043	$4,493,778	1.1	1.6	2.7
Middle States	176,768,399	3,054,576	3,217,485	6,272,061	2.7	1.8	3.5
Southern States..........	31,583,348	409,839	406,076	815,915	1.3	1.3	2.6
Western States and Terr's.	95,974,897	1,362,082	1,839,929	3,202,011	1.4	2.0	3.4
United States	471,064,238	6,727,232	8,056,533	14,783,765	1.4	1.7	3.1

1879.

New England States	$165,032,512	$1,942,209	$2,532,004	$4,474,213	1.2	1.5	2.7
Middle States	170,431,205	3,190,113	2,936,260	6,126,382	1.9	1.7	3.6
Southern States..........	30,555,018	425,997	383,927	809,924	1.4	1.3	2.7
Western States and Terr's.	90,949,769	1,457,812	1,751,032	3,208,844	1.6	2.0	3.6
United States	456,968,504	7,010,131	7,603,232	14,619,363	1.5	1.7	3.2

Cities.	Rates of taxation.								
	1877.			1878.			1879.		
	United States.	State.	Total.	United States.	State.	Total.	United States.	State.	Total.
	Per ct.	Per ct.	Per ct.	Per ct.	Per ct.	Per ct.	Per ct.	Per ct.	Per ct.
Boston	1.3	1.6	2.9	1.3	1.3	2.6	1.3	1.3	2.6
New York	2.1	2.9	5.0	2.2	2.9	5.1	2.6	2.9	5.5
Albany...................	3.0	3.2	6.2	2.8	2.8	5.6	2.9	2.5	5.4
Philadelphia	2.1	0.7	2.8	2.0	0.7	2.7	2.1	0.7	2.8
Pittsburgh	1.4	0.5	1.9	1.3	0.5	1.8	1.4	0.6	2.0
Baltimore	1.2	1.9	3.1	1.2	1.8	3.0	1.2	1.3	2.5
Washington	1.3	0.7	2.0	1.4	0.6	2.0	1.4	0.4	1.8
New Orleans	1.5	0.9	2.4	1.5	1.0	2.5	1.7	0.5	2.2
Louisville	1.4	0.5	1.9	1.4	0.5	1.9	1.5	0.6	2.1
Cincinnati...............	1.7	2.9	4.6	1.5	2.7	4.2	1.9	2.4	4.3
Cleveland	1.1	2.2	3.3	1.1	2.0	3.1	1.3	2.0	3.3
Chicago	2.2	2.9	5.8	2.5	2.6	5.1	3.4	2.4	5.8
Detroit..................	1.6	1.7	3.3	1.7	1.5	3.2	1.8	2.2	4.0
Milwaukee...............	2.4	2.6	5.0	2.4	2.6	5.0	2.8	2.5	5.3
Saint Louis..............	1.4	2.5	3.9	1.6	2.4	4.0	1.8	2.1	3.9
Saint Paul...............	1.3	1.7	3.0	1.3	1.5	2.8	1.5	1.5	3.0

The CHAIRMAN. The variations are caused by local taxation, and not by State taxation and United States taxation?

Mr. KNOX. Yes, sir.

Senator KERNAN. And the local taxes are much heavier than the State taxes?

Mr. KNOX. Yes, sir. These ratios are ratios on capital, and, of course, our ratios depend very much on the amounts of deposits. The deposits of a bank may be very much larger than its capital, and the United States taxes are levied upon its deposits; so that our ratios to capital with regard to taxation are not in all respects exactly fair, but in respect to State taxation they are strictly true.

Senator FERRY. Your report shows proportionately a very small amount of tax on capital, but largely on deposits and largely on circulation.

Senator ALLISON. Let me ask a question in regard to the tax on circulation, as bearing upon the cost of issuing notes. The tax on circulation is 1 per cent.?

Mr. KNOX. Yes, sir.

Senator ALLISON. Now, what is the actual cost of issuing these notes to the banks?

Mr. KNOX. It is said that you should keep up the tax on circulation, and one reason assigned for so doing is that the banks ought to pay all the cost of engraving and printing their notes, and all the expenses of my office. That is a proper thing to do, and the law as it passed originally provided that such costs and expenses should be paid out of this tax on circulation. That was one object of affixing the tax on circulation. But while the expenses of my office, including the paper, the engraving, the printing, and the issuing of all these notes, are about $200,000 a year, the government is the gainer by the single item of the loss in circulating notes of the banks to the extent of at least $3,500,000.

Senator MORRILL. Up to the present time?

Mr. KNOX. Up to this time about $3,500,000.

The CHAIRMAN. Has that amount disappeared?

Mr. KNOX. Yes, sir. That is profit to the government. That would pay the expenses of issuing the notes and everything connected with them for fifteen years.

Senator BECK. When do you expect the government to get that?

Mr. KNOX. In some cases there is only .75 of the circulation now outstanding.

Senator BECK. But we get nothing until final settlement with the bank.

Mr. KNOX. The government has the legal-tender notes all the while in its possession. It has the use of it continually.

Senator BECK. But what I want to get at is this: Will the banks be required to settle up and take in all the notes that were issued to them, whether lost or not, at the expiration of the charter or when do they expect to pay them?

Mr. KNOX. There are fifteen of the first banks that failed which now have a circulation outstanding of $11,628. It is an average of only .75 of one per cent. None of that will come in of any consequence. The government has gained $11,628 by the lost notes of these fifteen banks.

Senator BECK. Is it your understanding that at the expiration of the present charters of the banks they will each have to pay for all the circulation that was issued to them, and that then we shall get that profit and the loss?

Mr. KNOX. My understanding is that if a bank fails, discontinues business, or goes into liquidation, or if its charter expires, it must deposit lawful money in the Treasury for the full amount of its circulating notes.

Senator BECK. But its charter expires in twenty years, does it not?

Mr. KNOX. The limitation is twenty years.

Senator BECK. Is it expected that at the close of twenty years each bank will wind up and settle for all the circulation given to it, so as to give us the benefit of that loss?

Mr. KNOX. When a bank fails or goes into liquidation legal-tender notes are deposited on its account in the United States Treasury to the full amount of its outstanding circulation. The bank relinquishes all interest in or responsibility for this circulation by this deposit. The Treasury redeems or pays the bank notes. Some time must elapse, however, before the Treasury can tell in any particular case what amount of notes will never be presented. The notes which are never presented the government must finally gain, for it has for its own the legal tenders deposited in their place, but it also has a constant gain from the very first by the use of the legal tenders, which remain with it a longer or shorter time. Twenty-three banks which failed previous to 1873 have $45,644 of circulating notes still outstanding out of an original issue of $3,196,693. The proportion of the notes remaining unredeemed is, therefore, in the case of these banks, 1.43 per cent. of the amount issued. It is probable that further redemptions will reduce the percentage, which will never be redeemed, to about one per cent., as before stated. What the final gain will be can be judged from the results in the redemption of the notes of the first twenty-three banks.

Senator BECK. But you say we gain three and a half millions. We gain nothing until we get it; that is, our debt is not reduced until we settle with the banks. Is it proposed that each bank as its charter expires shall settle up and give us the benefit of that, or are they going to try to renew their charters again without accounting?

Mr. KNOX. It is impossible for the banks to go into liquidation without depositing in the Treasury legal tenders equal to the amount of their circulating notes. There is nothing in the law to prevent any national bank from going into liquidation at any time. There is nothing in the law to prevent any private persons from organizing a bank. If the national banks now in operation should see fit to go into liquidation they could do so, and thereafter the same stockholders could associate themselves together again, and organize another national bank.

Senator MORRILL. But the old notes would all have to be redeemed?

Mr. KNOX. Yes, sir.

The CHAIRMAN. Either redeemed or protected by a deposit of Treasury notes?

Mr. KNOX. Yes.

Senator BECK. But what I want to get at is, can they not do that for the purpose of preventing the twenty years' limitation running against them, and keep from paying us these three and a half millions?

Mr. KNOX. They must deposit Treasury notes to the amount of their circulation.

Senator BECK. And the government gets the benefit of the use of that money?

Mr. KNOX. Of that deposit fund, yes, sir.

Senator KERNAN. It becomes a new bank, to all intents and purposes, not a continuance in the sense of carrying along their old bills?

Mr. KNOX. Yes, sir.

Senator WALLACE. As the practical result of this fifth section on the question of refunding the national debt, I understand you to say it would amount to $60,000,000, and that to that extent it would change the circulation of the national banks?

Mr. KNOX. It would make a compulsory market for bonds to about that amount.

Senator WALLACE. That is the extent of it?

Mr. KNOX. Yes, sir; I shall be able to furnish the committee in a few days with the true figures.

Senator FERRY. And as to the $14,000,000 required as security for public moneys, that might make a place for bonds?

Mr. KNOX. In regard to that $14,000,000 it seems to me bad policy to say that the banks shall deposit only the lowest priced bond in the market as security for deposits. What the government wants is to get as much security as it can for its deposits. If there should be danger that these bonds would go below par, would not a bank hesitate about purchasing the bonds?

Senator FERRY. But the government should not hesitate to take its own bonds.

Mr. KNOX. But the bill says they shall buy only one class of bonds, and the bonds belong to the bank, and the government can decline to repurchase the bonds at par.

Senator KERNAN. You want to strike out "only," and let the banks furnish any bonds as security?

Mr. KNOX. I would let them deposit any bonds. It might diminish the amount of security to allow only 3-per cents. to be deposited. They might willingly purchase 4 per cents., or $3\frac{1}{2}$ per cents., but decline the depositary rather than invest in 3 per cents.

Senator ALLISON. I have not in my mind clearly your objections to the repeal of section 4 of the act of 1874 and the revival of these two sections of the Revised Statutes. Please repeat it.

Mr. KNOX. I think it deranges our present system, which is right as it is. After this funding bill is passed and the remainder of the debt refunded, there will be comparative stability in the price of bonds, and the repeal of section 4 will prevent the ebb and flow, the elasticity of the circulating note, which is indispensable to a well-regulated currency.

I want to refer to an objection made by Senator Beck. He referred yesterday to some abuses that may have grown up under this provision allowing banks to take up their bonds as they see fit. The Treasurer referred to it in his report, and I expected to have seen him here to-day.

Senator BECK. Allow me, before you go on. You remarked just now that the lowest-priced bonds ought not to be taken, because of the government seeking to give the best security to its depositors.

Mr. KNOX. Taking the best and largest amount of security for its deposits.

Senator BECK. The Secretary has the right to take other security besides bonds, if he thinks fit, under the present law.

Mr. KNOX. Under the present law, but not under the proposed section.

Senator BECK. Why not?

Mr. KNOX. I understand the section to mean that he shall receive only 3 per cent. bonds.

Senator BECK. Now let me ask again, upon that theory, why should this section of the law of 1874 stand, allowing them to have only $50,000 of bonds on deposit in such a case as that of the Bank of Missouri, we were talking about a while ago, if the government is looking to the interest of depositors? Is not the requirement of keeping one-third of their capital, under sections 5159 and 5160, a good deal better security for depositors than the present law that you now object to the repeal of?

Mr. KNOX. Our law is burdened with restrictions. I do not think there ever was an act put upon the statute book that had so many restrictions as the national-bank act.

Senator BECK. But the effect would be, would it not, under sections 5159 and 5160, that in the case we were discussing a while ago, if the Bank of Missouri had been required to comply with them she would have had $880,000 for the benefit of her depositors and stockholders as well, instead of $50,000 under the present law.

Mr. KNOX. She might have had more bonds.

Senator BECK. Would she not have been compelled to have?

Mr. KNOX. The character of assets depends on the men who transact the business—the board of directors.

Senator BECK. You say you want a high-priced bond for the security of depositors; do you not want one-third of the capital always deposited for security?

Mr. KNOX. I think the government would readily get a greater amount of security if the banks were at liberty to buy any United States bonds. The banks will generally keep one-third of their capital in bonds, but they should have the privilege to increase or decrease the circulation.

Senator BECK. Then why do you object to the reinstatement of those two sections?

Mr. KNOX. Because I do not think it is a good system.

Senator BECK. The Treasurer of the United States, on pages 19 and 21 of his report, which I now hand to you, and ask you to look over, goes on to show that gross abuses have grown up out of this act of 1874; for example:

Under the construction placed upon the law, banks which have thus reduced their circulation have been permitted to increase it again as often and as largely as they chose, whether their legal-tender deposits were exhausted or not. Although the exact amount cannot be ascertained, it is safe to say that many millions of dollars of additional circulation have been issued under the general provisions of the national currency act to banks which were still reducing their circulation under the act of June 20, 1874. The consequence has been that the new notes thus issued have, to a large extent, speedily been presented to the Treasury for redemption out of the legal-tender deposit. Banks which have applied in vain to the Treasurer for the surrender of their legal-tender deposits, have accomplished the same object by obtaining new circulation. The cost of printing the new notes thus issued is borne by the United States, so that the government, though not deriving the remotest benefit from the transaction, has been obliged to bear the whole expense of their issue, and a part of the expense of their redemption, simply to enable a bank to do by indirection what it was not permitted to do directly. In several instances banks have repeated the operation of reducing and increasing their circulation several times within a brief period, taking up their bonds and selling them, it would appear, whenever the premium constituted a sufficient inducement, and increasing their circulation again whenever bonds could be bought at better rates, the United States all the while redeeming their notes at its own expense or that of the other banks, and issuing others, also at its own expense, whenever called upon by them.

An example will better illustrate these operations. In January and February, 1875, a certain bank reduced its circulation from $308,490 to $45,000 by deposits of legal-tender notes. Between September 26, 1876, and May 26, 1877, and before that deposit was exhausted, it increased its circulation to $450,000. Between August 14 and September 10, 1877, it again reduced its circulation to $45,000. On September 19, 1877, nine days after completing the deposits for this reduction, it again began to take out additional circulation, although $402,550 of prior deposits remained in the Treasury, and by the 26th of that month its circulation had again been increased to $450,000. July 22, 1878, it, for the third time, reduced its circulation to $45,000, and in August and September, 1879, again increased it to $450,000, at which it now remains, the balance of its former legal-tender deposits then in the Treasury being $112,615. From January 13, 1875, to the date of this report, $778,275 of its notes have been redeemed, of which only $40,700 were redeemed at the expense of the bank, although during more than one-third of that period it had outstanding and was deriving the benefit from the full amount of circulation which its capital authorized. The only assessments which have been made on the bank for the expenses of redeeming its notes were $24.74 in 1875, and $4.39 in 1878. At one time there were in actual circulation $852,550 of its notes, although the highest amount ever borne on its books was $450,000.

That is what is possible, and what is done under the act of 1874, which is sought to be repealed, and is impossible under the sections of the statutes sought to be revived. Against this repeal and revival the Comptroller protests, and for this the Secretary pleads. I want the Comptroller to tell why he pleads for that system. If I was an agent of a bank, I would plead for it, but as a public officer I cannot understand how it can be done.

The CHAIRMAN. Do I understand that any portion of this $852,550 was secured by 100 per cent. of bonds against 90 per cent. of notes?

Senator BECK. I think not, and I want the Treasurer here to explain it, and I want Mr. Knox now to state why it is right.

The CHAIRMAN. It is a very important fact.

Senator **Beck**. I think I shall show that it is all wrong, and that this section, of the act of 1874, ought to be repealed, and these sections of the statutes ought to be revived, in spite of the Comptroller. It is for the interest of the banks and against the people.

Mr. **Knox**. I called on the Treasurer this morning, on my way here, in the hope that he would come with me, and aid in explaining this matter to your satisfaction.

Senator **Beck**. Explain it, if you please, and we shall get him to explain it, too. Is that report of his true?

Mr. **Knox**. In the first place, the law provides that the banks shall have bonds on deposit to the amount of their circulation, and 10 per cent. more; but if a bank wishes to reduce its circulation from $200,000 to $150,000, it deposits $50,000 in legal-tender notes and takes out a proportionate amount of its bonds. The bank has then no more interest in those $50,000 of its notes which it has redeemed than you, or I, or any outsider has. The government has the legal-tender notes on deposit to redeem the bank notes. If there is anybody that receives any benefit resulting from the circulation of those notes, it is the government. According to the Treasurer's statement of November 1 last, the amount of legal tenders lying in the Treasury deposited by banks which had gone into voluntary liquidation, or by associations desiring to reduce their circulation, was about $20,000,000.

Senator **Beck**. Do you say the system is good that enables that to be done which the Treasurer says is being done?

Mr. **Knox**. I wish to say that no bank has any circulation outstanding in excess of 90 per cent. of the bonds on deposit therefor, that it has any interest in, or from which it derives any profit whatever.

Senator **Beck**. But do you know what bank is referred to there by the Treasurer?

Mr. **Knox**. I really do not know. I suppose I might guess.

Senator **Beck**. What is your best guess?

Mr. **Knox**. I suppose it is in reference to a bank in the city of New York. I do not know that it is.

Senator **Beck**. Which one do you think it is?

Mr. **Knox**. I suppose it is the First National Bank of New York.

Senator **Beck**. I rather think so from the amounts. Do you say that that bank had in the Treasury, when it had $880,000 of circulation, $880,000 of bonds with 10 per cent. more?

Mr. **Knox**. Either in bonds or in legal tender notes.

Senator **Beck**. If it had $480,000 of bonds and $400,000 of legal-tender notes it was locking up that much of legal-tender money.

Mr. **Knox**. It was so much additional legal-tender in the Treasury.

Senator **Beck**. When it wanted to redeem, why should it not bring in its own notes, as provided by these two sections 5159 and 5160, instead of keeping its old notes out and getting new ones too?

Mr. **Knox**. If you will look at the Treasurer's currency balance on November 1, you will see that it was $26,000,000 only, of which amount $20,000,000 consisted of legal-tender notes deposited by the national banks for the purpose of retiring their own notes.

Senator **Beck**. Does not the government have to print new notes every time there is an increase in circulation made by a bank?

Mr. **Knox**. We have national-bank notes in our vaults all the time already printed. When these are exhausted new notes must, of course, be printed.

Senator **Beck**. And the United States prints them, and pays the expense of them?

4 N D

Mr. KNOX. Yes, sir. Let me say what, in my opinion, will be the probable action of the banks if this bill should go into operation. The condition of affairs that has arisen within the last two years as a result of the recent refunding operations is unprecedented. We have had a most extraordinary situation in the city of New York, as well as elsewhere. The 4 per cent. bonds of the government, which only about two years ago sold at par or at 102, have increased in value until they now sell for 112 or 113. All classes of the unmatured bonds of the United States have borne large premiums. In the city of New York a bank which is receiving 1½ per cent. a year of profit upon its circulation, finding the premium upon its bonds to be 10 or 12 per cent., naturally would like to realize that premium, and therefore it would probably substitute legal-tender notes and dispose of its bonds in the market. This state of affairs will not long continue after the refunding operations shall have been completed.

We have had two kinds of 5 per cent. and five or six kinds of 6 per cent. bonds, together with 4 and 4½ per cents; all this variety of bonds in the market. The market has been unsettled; that is, it has been rising, and there has been a great profit on the buying and selling of bonds. Banks bought them low and now sell them high. Many banks have suffered losses, and the rise in the value of the bonds has helped to meet these losses. But after these present bonds have been negotiated, and refunding operations shall have been completed, there will not be any such range in the price of bonds.

Senator BECK. Perhaps not; but if the act of 1874 makes this thing possible, and the re-enactment of those two sections makes the banks redeem their own notes and makes it impossible, is it not safer and better for the country that it should be so than to keep up a condition of things that made that statement of the Treasurer true?

Mr. KNOX. If the banks are required and permitted to deposit 3½ per cent. bonds only as security for circulation, the transaction of which you complain would then of necessity cease. If the tax were reduced to one-half of one per cent. upon circulation issued on 3½ per cent. bonds only, or on bonds bearing interest at, say, 3.30, it would in my opinion result in making a market for not less than $360,000,000 of such bonds at par or above. I wish to say further, in regard to the Treasurer's statement, that there has been no additional expense to the Government of the United States by the operation. He says there were expenses to the other banks or to the Treasury. The expense has been almost entirely, you might say, $\frac{9}{10}$ or $\frac{4}{5}$ at the expense of the other banks and not at the expense of the Treasury.

Senator BECK. But why should the other banks be required to pay for the change made three or four different times, and new notes be issued every time printed by the Treasury and furnished to those gentlemen when their own notes were still outstanding?

Mr. KNOX. There is a defect in the law in this respect, which is pointed out at page 56 of my last report.

Senator BECK. I think so.

Mr. KNOX. The law provides that the banks shall pay the expense of redeeming their notes, but the government, in my opinion, should properly pay the expense of retiring the notes of liquidating and insolvent banks, for the money is permanently deposited in the Treasury for that purpose. But there being no law authorizing this to be done, the Treasurer is obliged to collect from the banks in operation the cost of redeeming the notes of the banks in liquidation or that are retiring their circulation.

The CHAIRMAN. Still there was an equal opportunity to all banks to do this thing?

Mr. KNOX. Of course. It is a mere temporary thing.

Senator WALLACE. The theory of this system in your mind, Mr. Knox, is. that the government should have entire control only of the security for circulation.

Mr. KNOX. That is my theory.

Senator WALLACE. Is it the disposition of the banking department of the United States Treasury to tend to that result?

Mr. KNOX. So far as the deposit of bonds is concerned. There are other restrictions on the act that the Chairman has referred to in reference to reserves which are the result of experience.

Senator WALLACE. I am looking to the other question, the question of principle. Is it the tendency of the banking department of the United States to absorb the control of the banking interests, or only of the security for circulation?

Mr. KNOX. That is all, the security for circulation.

Senator WALLACE. In other words, you are willing, so far as you can, to permit each individual bank to stand on its own good management, except so far as the security of the note-holder is concerned?

Mr. KNOX. That is it exactly.

The CHAIRMAN. Is there any possible means under existing law by which a note unsecured by a ratio of 100 to 90 per cent. of the United States bonds deposited can be issued by a bank?

Mr. KNOX. It can never occur.

Senator BECK. One more question there. In the case put by the Treasurer, was there a dollar more than legal-tender notes of an equal number of the notes of the bank outstanding in the Treasury for any sum beyond $440,000?

Mr. KNOX. No, sir.

Senator BECK. Then there was no 10 per cent. additional to secure that $440,000, half of the $880,000?

Mr. KNOX. Dollar for dollar in legal-tender notes.

Senator BECK. That was all. There was no percentage?

Mr. KNOX. No.

Senator BECK. And no bonds?

The CHAIRMAN. What had become of the bonds then?

Mr. KNOX. The bank, for instance, had $450,000 of circulation and $500,000 of bonds.

Senator BECK. And never more at any time?

Mr. KNOX. That was all. It saw fit to withdraw $200,000 of its bonds, and then some days or weeks thereafter to buy new bonds and deposit them, upon which we gave them circulation. We would not have given them this circulation if the Treasurer had been willing to return to them the legal-tender notes which they had deposited. This he could have done. There was no law to prevent it.

Senator BECK. That bank might have sent its own notes to Minnesota, so that they could not get back for a year, and get other notes from the Treasury. It actually had $880,000 of its own notes outstanding, and never had but $500,000 in bonds on deposit here.

Mr. KNOX. You have a wrong impression about it.

The CHAIRMAN. I see that under the provision which enables these banks to go into liquidation, where they cannot get back their own notes from any cause, they are allowed to deposit United States notes dollar for dollar, and be relieved. It was that permission, as I understand, at all times to account for the national-bank circulation by buying United States Treasury notes, under which the bank in question did buy, say, a thousand or a million of United States Treasury notes, and put them in the Treasury, as if it had retired its own notes.

Senator BECK. The bonds should be there for the protection of any demands for the payment of those notes all the time; and therefore they had by the same law a right to deposit new bonds and draw the 90 per cent. of circulation upon the new bonds.

Mr. KNOX. There is no advantage, whatever, to any bank in a transaction of this kind, except the realizing of the premium upon its bonds. That is all.

Senator ALLISON. Did it buy the same bonds back at a lower rate?

Mr. KNOX. It could either buy the same bonds or other bonds at a lower rate.

Senator BECK. You find on the Treasurer's books two sets of accounts, one running up and the other down, see-sawing, on these bonds.

Senator FERRY. I want to put one question. Has there ever been a loss to the holder of a national-bank note or a legal-tender note during your administration?

The CHAIRMAN. There has been a loss of legal-tenders by the premium on gold.

Senator FERRY. I mean the par value.

Mr. KNOX. No loss, except where parties have lost the notes themselves.

Senator FERRY. I refer to the payment.

Mr. KNOX. O, no.

The CHAIRMAN. What effect would a reduction of taxes have on the negotiation of the new bonds?

Mr. KNOX. The tax upon the deposits of the national banks for the year 1880 was four millions, and the tax on the deposits of State and savings banks and private banks was two and one-half millions. The tax upon capital for all classes of banks was nearly $1,200,000. The tax on deposits is imposed not only on national banks but on all the other banks and bankers of the country—nearly 4,000 in number. It is very unfair in its operation. Frequently the same original deposit is assessed three or four times in as many different places. The repeal of this tax would have the tendency to increase the profits of the banks and decrease the rate of interest. There is so much competition in banking, and money is so plenty at the present time, that the rates of interest are not likely in any event to go beyond the legal rate. This repeal would, if anything could do so under the present low profit on circulation, induce the organization of new banks and cause some additional demand for the bonds.

The tax on capital has had the effect to largely decrease the banking capital of the country. The capital of the national banks in March, 1876, was 504 millions; on October 1, 1880, it was 457 millions. The number of banks in existence at the former date was 2,091, and at the latter 2,090, and yet the decrease in capital was 47 millions. The capital of State banks and private bankers in 1876 was 214 millions, and in 1880 190 millions, showing a decrease of 24 millions. A considerable portion of this reduction in the capital of all classes of banks has occurred since the date of resumption, notwithstanding the great increase of business since that date. This is owing largely to State taxation, but the repeal of the government taxes on capital and deposits would give some relief and would induce all classes of banks and bankers, amounting to more than 6,500, to favorably consider the new loan. The reduction of one-half the tax on circulation issued on the new bonds only would have a directly favorable effect on the sale of bonds, and, as I have already said, would, in my opinion, furnish a market for 360 millions of bonds bearing interest, say, at 3 30, all of which bonds would be permanently held by the banks as security for circulating notes.

FRIDAY, *January* 28, 1881.

The committee resumed its session, there being present, besides the members of the committee, Hon. James Gilfillan, Treasurer of the United States.

The CHAIRMAN. Mr. Gilfillan, you may proceed to make your comment upon the funding bill, or that portion of it which embraces the 5th section. A copy of the bill is before you.

Mr. GILFILLAN. I was not informed in the notice to appear of any particular point upon which a statement from me was desired.

The CHAIRMAN. I believe that it was on the suggestion of Mr. Beck that Mr. Gilfillan was asked to come before the committee.

Senator BECK. The reason why I made the suggestion that perhaps induced the chairman to call Mr. Gilfillan's attention more particularly to the 5th section was that when we had Mr. Knox before us I read from the report of the Treasurer, on pages 19, 20, and 21, showing the bad effects, as I think, of some of the provisions of the act of 1874, suggesting a return to the act of 1864, or sections 5159 and 5160 of the Revised Statutes. I said I would be very anxious to hear the Treasurer as to the operations of these banks in increasing and reducing and reducing and increasing, backwards and forwards. No doubt that is why the chairman called the attention of Mr. Gilfillan more particularly to that section at first. Here is your report, Mr. Gilfillan. which contains the general history and operation of the system, and how far the 5th section seems to remedy the evils you speak of there, was the point I was endeavoring to obtain.

Mr. GILFILLAN. The Treasurer is made the custodian, and holds in trust the bonds deposited for circulation of the national banks. Under the act of June 20, 1874, he is also required to redeem the circulation of all national banks when presented.

The CHAIRMAN. On page 19 of your report, speaking of the reduction and increase of national-bank circulation, you say that the law of June 20, 1874, "authorizes any national bank desiring to withdraw its circulating notes to take up the bonds deposited for the security of such notes upon the deposit of lawful money"—which means United States notes—"with the Treasurer of the United States, and provides that an equal amount of the outstanding notes of the bank shall be redeemed at the Treasury" when they are presented.

The statement you make is, that the entire expense of the redemption of the whole of this large amount which has been brought in has been borne by other national banks, and you state the object of this deposit of United States notes, in order to take up the currency which has been secured by the deposit of bonds, has been, on the part of the banks, not to increase their volume of currency, but it has been to avail themselves of the premium upon their bonds by a sale. Let me ask you what would be the actual expense if each bank for such operation as that were to pay itself the expense of transfer and exchange of the money; could they not diminish the expense very much by having notes of very large denominations issued to them instead of small ones ?

Mr. GILFILLAN. Yes, sir; the expense of assorting would be reduced in that way.

The CHAIRMAN. What is the whole expense of that bureau?

Mr. GILFILLAN. Last year it was $143,728.39.

Senator MORRILL. Less than it has been before?

Mr. GILFILLAN. Yes, sir; nearly $100,000 less than the preceding year. It cost each bank of $100,000 capital, with $90,000 circulation, $37.69 to have such of its notes redeemed as were presented for redemption during the last fiscal year.

The CHAIRMAN. You illustrate this by stating that a certain bank, to which you refer on page 20, twice repeated the operation of depositing $450,000. That would be $900,000. What would be the actual expense of that if the bank had borne it by itself?

Mr. GILFILLAN. The expense of assorting would have been computed by the one thousand notes; the expense of transportation by the one thousand dollars.

Senator KERNAN. What was the expense of each operation?

The CHAIRMAN. The actual expense?

Senator KERNAN. Which would be repeated.

Mr. GILFILLAN. There would be first the expense of paper and printing the notes, which is borne by the United States.

The CHAIRMAN. What would that amount to?

Mr. GILFILLAN. I do not know the exact cost, but it would not be less than $1,550 for that amount of notes of average denominations.

The CHAIRMAN. Would not a great deal of that expense depend upon the denominations that were asked for?

Mr. GILFILLAN. Yes, sir; it would depend entirely upon that.

The CHAIRMAN. Does it cost more to print a note for $1,000 than one for $10?

Mr. GILFILLAN. No; the expense is usually reckoned by the thousand sheets; it costs so much a sheet, whether the note is a dollar note, or a thousand dollar note, or a ten thousand dollar note.

The CHAIRMAN. The mere matter of printing?

Mr. GILFILLAN. Precisely.

The CHAIRMAN. Could you estimate what the expense to the government was of the transfer of eight or nine hundred thousand dollars?

Mr. GILFILLAN. Not with exactness, without knowing the denominations of the notes and the number.

Senator KERNAN. Could you give us per sheet about how much it would be, whether a one dollar note or a hundred dollar note?

Mr. GILFILLAN. The difficulty in estimating the cost of national bank notes is that different denominations are printed on the same sheet. It is different with United States notes.

The CHAIRMAN. But this has nothing to do with United States notes, except when they have brought them back and deposited them. It is the cost of the national currency.

Mr. GILFILLAN. I have nothing to do with the issue of national bank notes, and I do not know definitely as to the cost.

The CHAIRMAN. You have referred in your report to the expense of that as having been incurred at the cost of the whole association of banks, when in this particular case an individual bank had all the benefit of it?

Mr. GILFILLAN. Yes, sir. Reducing banks under existing law have the benefit and escape the expense.

The CHAIRMAN. I should like to know, after all, what was the cost; if it amounted to a great deal of money?

Mr. GILFILLAN. I cannot tell the exact cost without knowing the denomination of the notes.

The CHAIRMAN. Was it very serious?

Mr. GILFILLAN. The expense last year of redeeming $900,000 of bank notes of average denominations was $2,340, to which should be added $1,550, the estimated cost of paper and printing.

Senator KERNAN. I do not quite understand how frequent operations like that mentioned on page 21 of your report occur. I want to get at the fact, whether that was a frequent thing.

The CHAIRMAN. As I understand the cost to the bureau in redemption, it amounts to $143,000 a year, about $37 on every bank having a circulation of $90,000. One of these banks, however, returns as a circulation, you may say, in the same year, $900,000 by these means. I merely want to know whether that is a very serious cost, and becomes a matter of serious injustice to the association of banks for the individual return of its circulation twice over?

Mr. GILFILLAN. The cases in my report were only cited as illustrations. There has been under the act of June 20, 1874, $71,000,000 retired, but the net decrease in national-bank circulation outstanding has only been about $7,000,000 since the passage of that act. It was not the cost to any particular bank, but the system under which such transactions take place, to which the attention of the department was invited.

Senator MORRILL. Was this surrendering of currency resorted to to any great extent throughout the country?

Mr. GILFILLAN. I do not know how many banks did it.

Senator KERNAN. It is not surrendering currency. They deposit greenbacks to redeem, say, $50,000 of their own bills, and then they do not take up their bonds. Their bonds are there, and then they just take out, two days after, the same amount of bank notes again which they have prepared to redeem. Is that it?

The CHAIRMAN. No.

Senator KERNAN. Let me read from the Treasurer's Report, on page 21:

Other banks have reduced and forthwith increased their circulation to its former amount, with the avowed object of relieving themselves from the trouble and expense of redeeming their notes through the five per cent. redemption fund. For example, a bank deposited $45,000 in legal-tender notes for the reduction of its circulation on April 3, 1878, and on April 5, 1878, two days afterwards, without having touched the bonds deposited as security, took out $45,000 of additional circulation. In like manner on July 11, 1879, it deposited $9,000 for the same purpose, and on the very same day, without disturbing its bonds, it took out $9,000 of additional circulation.

Do you not see that the government has the trouble of redeeming these notes and then putting right out the same amount?

Senator MORRILL. But they have the same amount. The government has it in advance.

Senator KERNAN. They have their regular notes there.

Senator MORRILL. So that the bank does not get a dollar more?

Senator KERNAN. That is so; but the Treasurer is speaking in his report about their speculating in stocks, taking the ups and downs of stocks and contracting the currency by depositing greenbacks and waiting for notes or getting new notes, contracting it to that extent in hard times. That is the purport of the statement, and I want to know if there is much of that done?

Senator MORRILL. I suppose the point you are trying to get at is the case of a bank with some 4½ per cents on deposit that are bringing a high premium. They want to sell those and get some others in that they can get at less expense.

Senator KERNAN. The Treasurer says they did this " with the avowed object of relieving themselves from the trouble and expense of redeeming their notes through the 5 per cent. redemption fund." In a word, they throw it on the government. Now, whether much or little, they should not do that.

Mr. GILFILLAN. The Treasurer's statement was made not to draw attention to any particular banks, but to the system. Of course, a contingency might arise under which the evil would be greatly increased. That was the point, and not merely to call attention to the evil as it has existed in the past.

The CHAIRMAN. Repeat that statement, please.

Mr. GILFILLAN. Not merely that there has been improper fluctuation of circulation in the past, but contingencies may arise in funding which will induce the banks to reduce circulation largely. There are seven hundred and fifty banks which now have but $50,000 capital. They cannot reduce under the fourth section of the act of 1874. It might happen that those seven hundred and fifty banks would be left to bear the expense of redeeming the notes of all the national banks.

The CHAIRMAN. I see that your comment, at pages 19 and 20, is that the apparent intention of the act of June 20, 1874, was to allow this power to banks of returning United States notes to the Treasury and taking out their bonds, and in that way retiring their own circulation ; for when they have deposited United States notes they are exonerated from any responsibility for the circulation issued to them by the government, whether it is outstanding or not. It was thought that it would be what you may call a regulation of the volume of currency; that when it became redundant they could retire their currency; when they desired more currency they could deposit more bonds and issue more currency; but that, under the working of the system, has been simply to enable them to avail themselves of the fluctuations in the price of bonds; and not for the purpose of checking a redundancy of currency, but for the purpose merely of obtaining the premium upon the bonds they have availed themselves of this act, bringing United States notes in when they could not get their own, and taking up their bonds for the purpose of sale.

Mr. GILFILLAN. The higher the market rate of bonds the less elastic the currency would be—if it is ever elastic under that section, which is doubtful—because the bank can only get the same amount of circulation on a bond worth 150 as on a bond at par, so that if it were elastic when bonds are at par, when they get to be at a high rate of premium it may be for the interest of a bank to look to the premium on the bonds and not to the profit on circulation. That is the point.

Senator ALLISON. Do you say that under this funding bill this operation might be carried on to a large extent, you think ?

Mr. GILFILLAN. Yes, sir; under circumstances which might arise.

Senator ALLISON. They would carry it on in this way, would they not ? They would take out their 4 per cent. bonds, deriving a large premium for the time being by the deposit of greenbacks, and then after a little while they would buy the 3½ or 3 per cent. bonds and take circulation upon those ? Is not that your idea of the way it would operate ?

Mr. GILFILLAN. When that part of my report was written, of course I had neither funding operations nor this bill in view.

Senator ALLISON. You had in view an amendment to the bank act ?

Mr. GILFILLAN. Or a regulation of the department, if it could be effected in that way.

Senator ALLISON. The object to the banks, as I understand these pages in your report, is to take out bonds bearing a large premium?

Mr. GILFILLAN. That seems to be the object.

Senator ALLISON. And if they would do it to a considerable extent under this funding bill they would do it by selling their high-priced bonds and buying the low-priced bonds that we propose to sell. Is not that the way they would exert themselves?

Mr. GILFILLAN. They might, unless they wished to absolutely surrender the circulation entirely.

Senator ALLISON. So that this provision would really aid the funding operations rather than retard them? In other words, if I understand your statement correctly, the revival of these two sections of the Revised Statutes, and the repeal of section 4, might have the effect to retard the operations of the remainder of this bill, to wit, an inducement for the banks to take low-priced bonds instead of high-priced bonds?

Mr. GILFILLAN. Perhaps so, on that supposition, which is improbable, because under existing law banks can reduce their bonds to $30,000 without substituting others, but if the 5th section is enacted they must substitute the new bonds to an amount equal to one-third of their capital.

Senator ALLISON. Then, is it not true that, while we are engaged in this operation of funding, it would be wise to postpone a change of this bank law until that was done?

Mr. GILFILLAN. As to any other direct effect on funding, I am not prepared to speak. I am only incidentally interested in the question as it affects the business of the Treasurer's office, which will be benefited by the proposed change in the system.

Senator ALLISON. I understand; but I understood you to say that this might be done largely under this funding bill. If so, I want to see how it would be done.

Mr. GILFILLAN. I spoke of the fact that reduction of bank circulation might take place, and throw the expense of redeeming the notes on a few banks; that is all.

Senator ALLISON. Undoubtedly.

Mr. GILFILLAN. As to what effect the repeal of section 4 of the act of 1874 would have on funding, other than that such repeal will tend to retard sharp contraction of the currency and withdrawal of bonds, I am not prepared to say.

The CHAIRMAN. Were your remarks influenced by the fact of an increased expense that you thought was caused by individual banks at the cost of the entire association of banks? Was that the view with which this was written?

Mr. GILFILLAN. That and the expense to the United States of printing the notes.

The CHAIRMAN. Was your comment with a view of the effect of this law on the refunding question or not?

Mr. GILFILLAN. No, sir. I had not that in mind at the time of writing.

Senator ALLISON. I see that the two examples that you cite are examples that occurred in 1877, 1878, and 1879. Have there been any notable examples of this character during the last year?

Mr. GILFILLAN. I did not look at that. I will answer that question before this statement is completed. I have not the figures at this moment.

Senator ALLISON. I should like to have an answer. I should like to know if this is a continuous operation, because I can see very well how it would occur during the process of funding before. The banks that had high-priced bonds would draw them in and sell them and then buy in the 4's and renew their circulation.

Senator WALLACE. The effect of that would be to throw a great many 4's on the market and renew the operation to take up the currency.

Senator ALLISON. No; because the common market would absorb them anyway.

Senator WALLACE. That is the question.

Senator ALLISON. It would, because their number is limited.

Mr. GILFILLAN. During the fiscal year 1880, additional circulation was issued to two hundred and two national banks, thirty-one of which banks had legal-tender notes on deposit in the Treasury for the reduction of their circulation. Since July 1, 1880, additional circulation has been issued to thirty-six national banks, twelve of which banks had legal-tender notes on deposit in the Treasury for the reduction of their circulation.

Senator MORRILL. I understand that Mr. Gilfillan in making the report mainly referred to the injustice that he thought was done to some of the other banks in throwing the entire expense upon the associated banks instead of defraying it themselves, as it was an operation in which a single bank was exclusively interested.

The CHAIRMAN. It goes further than that. On page 21 you will see he says that there has been an operation under this law that never was contemplated. After speaking of the fact of the sudden return of the currency, and then the sudden demand for more, he says:

Such a construction utterly perverts the original intention of the act. Instead of the volume of the circulation being regulated by the business needs of the country it is governed by the price of United States bonds. The price of bonds may be such as to induce banks to surrender their circulation at the very time when there is a legitimate demand for more circulation.

That is rather a wider scope of his remark than confines it merely to the question of unjust expense thrown by the operations of one bank upon the entire association of banks.

Mr. GILFILLAN. There is no doubt that the elasticity of currency, as it is called, is affected by the premium on the bonds.

Senator ALLISON. There is no doubt of that; I can see that.

Mr. GILFILLAN. As to whether premium governs to a large extent, you will see on page 35 of the Treasurer's report that during the fiscal year 1880, $24,973,950 of 4 per cent. bonds were withdrawn. The desire to realize premium had a great deal to do with the withdrawal of these 4 per cent. bonds. In order to obtain the bonds to sell they were forced to reduce the circulation or directly substitute other bonds.

The CHAIRMAN. What is the remedy you would suggest for that?

Mr. GILFILLAN. When the paragraph was written it was not in expectation that there would be a change in the law, but that there might be some regulation of the department adopted that a bank should not increase its circulation while it was on the books of the department as reducing its circulation.

The CHAIRMAN. At page 22 you suggest to "confine the operation of the fourth section of the act of June 20, 1874, to cases where banks had formed a well-considered intention to permanently curtail their circulation, and would relieve the United States from the expense of issuing notes to banks only to have them forthwith returned for destruction." Would not that very fact, permanently curtailing the circulation, destroy the very feature of elasticity which is intended to be a measure of temporary relief? That is to say, you have more currency when more currency is needed, and retire it when its use becomes less profitable.

Mr. GILFILLAN. Then the only question is whether the volume of notes redeemed by the Treasurer, which has averaged $170,000,000 annually under section 3 of the act of 1874, would be great enough for the purposes of the national banks desiring to reduce their circulation.

The CHAIRMAN. If there be a deposit of United States Treasury notes to await the redemption of national currency which is sought to be retired there is no change in the volume at all?

Mr. GILFILLAN. Of course the United States notes that are deposited are immediately taken out of the circulation of the country.

The CHAIRMAN. Do you hold, therefore, that there is an increased volume in the circulating medium by the operation that you have described here of the banking?

Mr. GILFILLAN. An increase?

The CHAIRMAN. That is to say, if a bank having $100,000 of circulating notes, for which United States bonds have been deposited as security, desiring to take up those bonds for any purpose, for sale or otherwise, brings $100,000 of Treasury notes and deposits them, that entitles it to two things, to a return of the bonds that it deposited originally as security, and to exoneration from any liability for its outstanding currency. Is not that the result?

Mr. GILFILLAN. Yes, sir.

The CHAIRMAN. Then the United States notes deposited in lieu of, and I will say for the redemption of the national-bank currency, are immediately issued again by the Treasurer, or do they await as a fund the redemption of the outstanding notes of that bank as the notes delivered to that bank by the government?

Mr. GILFILLAN. Those identical notes might be paid out, but in paying those out of course the same amount of money of some other kind is retained.

The CHAIRMAN. That is what I wanted to know, whether when a bank returned $100,000 of Treasury notes to the Treasury, and obtained thereby the bonds that had been deposited as security for the circulation issued to them under the form of a bank, that bank circulation would be still outstanding?

Mr. GILFILLAN. Yes, sir.

The CHAIRMAN. But the $100,000 Treasury notes would be held to cancel it so far as the bank was concerned?

Mr. GILFILLAN. Yes, sir.

The CHAIRMAN. But that $100,000 would be retained as a fund for the ultimate redemption of that amount?

Mr. GILFILLAN. Yes, sir.

The CHAIRMAN. And never issued?

Mr. GILFILLAN. Never issued, but held as a fund. We do not speak now of the identical money. The fund is always there.

The CHAIRMAN. Then there is no increase of circulation by means of this exchange, but there may be a diminution when it is a permanent retirement of the notes?

Mr. GILFILLAN. Yes, sir. What was meant by permanent intention to reduce is that banks should not increase before their deposit of United States notes was exhausted.

Senator KERNAN. That is, if they did then issue other bonds to get $100,000 more of currency, and put that out, that would increase the currency to some extent.

Mr. GILFILLAN. That would increase the currency, but if they had deposited $50,000 of United States notes to retire circulation, they should wait until $50,000 of their notes was retired before they are granted an increase of circulation.

Senator KERNAN. Why should they do that? If there is need of more currency what harm is it? Where is the objection?

Mr. GILFILLAN. There is not any objection if it is done legitimately; but that would be to a small extent probably.

Senator ALLISON. Suppose $10,000 of this $50,000 had been redeemed; suppose this $50,000 fund for instance had been reduced to $40,000, then would it not be fair and legitimate for a bank to step in and deposit bonds enough to take $10,000 more of currency?

Mr. GILFILLAN. There might be less objection to that.

Senator ALLISON. In other words, your idea is that they should not have $50,000 of circulation represented by United States notes in the Treasury, and $50,000 more circulation out?

Mr. GILFILLAN. Yes, sir.

Senator ALLISON. But if they reduce their circulation by redemptions in the Treasury to that extent there would be no objection?

Mr. GILFILLAN. No objection if the reducing bank shared in the expense. The retirement of the circulation, if all the notes that came in for redemption under the third section of the act were canceled, would be very rapid. You see it has averaged $170,000,000 a year during the last six years, or nearly half of the outstanding national-bank circulation annually. The question is whether that is not as rapid as the public interests would permit the circulation to be curtailed. It might not suit an individual bank; its notes might not come in rapidly enough, but any general reduction of the circulation could be made that way very rapidly.

The CHAIRMAN. I have always understood that the great and fundamental protection of the interposition of a system of banks between the Treasury and the public was in the fact that when a paper currency became redundant it was in the power of the bank to retire it, but the government could not; that the bank could and would retire it under the exigencies of commercial demand and supply; no matter what may be the motive for the banks, the fact of the sudden and vacillating premiums upon the bonds, has induced them, it seems, at this time alone, to retire the currency for the purpose of getting hold of the bonds, in order to avail themselves of the premium by a sale; but the question is whether you suggest, and whether it is wise, that you should take from the bank, the power of retiring currency by returning it to the Treasury, and taking up their bonds whenever they find that that currency cannot be profitably used under the exigencies of commercial demand.

Mr. GILFILLAN. That is the point, whether aside from the redemption by the Treasury of their circulation the banks also need this other method, which is furnished by the fourth section of the act of June 20, 1874, to enable them to reduce more rapidly than can be done by the ordinary redemption through the Treasurer's office.

Senator MORRILL. Is it not a convenience and a great benefit to the country when the cotton is to be moved, when the corn crop is to be moved, out West, that there should be some power on the part of the banks to increase their circulation, and then at other seasons of the year, for seven or eight months when they do not want it, to retire it? If this system allows that to be done is it not of some public benefit?

Mr. GILFILLAN. That is the legitimate object of section 4, but in its practical working it fails; the so-called elasticity is restricted by the fact that banks are not willing generally to expend funds in their possession to buy bonds at a premium in order to get a less amount in circulation for the convenience of the country, and have not done so. This last summer there was a demand for circulation, which was not supplied by the banks, and the Treasury was compelled to issue over $30,000,000 of silver certificates and add to the circulation of the country.

Senator KERNAN. And silver dollars?

Senator MORRILL. But if we had refunded, and the bonds became stable, so that there would not be any greater fluctuation than there is in English consols, would not this principle in the existing laws be of some service to the country?

Mr. GILFILLAN. Doubtless, the nearer bonds are to par the more stable the circulation will be.

Senator WALLACE. Would not that stability follow naturally from the fact that only one class of bonds bearing one rate of interest were attainable by the national banks for the purpose of obtaining circulation; a class of bonds that would sell at or near par, and would pay the world's rate of interest? Would not that tend to bring that stability?

Mr. GILFILLAN. Yes, sir; it would tend to bring stability.

Senator KERNAN. In other words, they would hardly be tempted to refrain from getting circulation when it was needed, if there was a bond in the market that was always not much above par.

Senator WALLACE. And if that bond was the only bond the bank could deposit for circulation.

Senator KERNAN. Supposing it was not the only bond, it would be the low one, the one they would take, being so much lower than the others.

Senator ALLISON. Can a bank now, under the operations of the Treasury, having bonds bearing 4 per cent. interest, say, apply to the Treasury for the privilege of withdrawing 4 per cents, and substitute therefor, without reference to the currency, 4½ per cents?

Mr. GILFILLAN. Yes, sir; under section 5167, Revised Statutes.

Senator ALLISON. That exchange of bonds can go on, leaving their currency as it stands?

Mr. GILFILLAN. Yes, sir.

Senator ALLISON In other words, if a bank holding 4 per cent. bonds as security for circulation, after this funding bill shall become a law, desired to withdraw those 4's, could they do so and substitute, the 3½'s or 3's without any disturbance of their circulation?

Mr. GILFILLAN. Yes, sir.

Senator ALLISON. That process can go on.

Mr. GILFILLAN. It is going on all the time.

Senator ALLISON. They are exchanging one class of bonds for another bond.

Mr. GILFILLAN. One bond for another, whenever a bank makes the request.

Senator ALLISON. I wanted to know if that was under the regular operation of the Treasury. Of course that seems to be a very wise provision.

Senator BECK. I should like to ask whether you have seen any occasion to modify the recommendations of your report in regard to the reduction and increase of national-bank circulation on pages 19, 20, and 21 of the report, and, if so, in what regard would you modify the statements therein made, or are the facts therein stated according to your understanding yet true?

Mr. GILFILLAN. They are true, and I see no reason to modify them now.

Senator BECK. You gave an illustration at the top of page 21, where, under the process of contracting and expanding at various times, you say:

At one time there were in actual circulation—

Of the bank which you use as an illustration—

$852,550 of its notes, although the highest amount ever borne on its books was $450,000.

Mr. GILFILLAN. That is a true statement.

Senator BECK. Was there ever at any time more than $500,000 of bonds deposited by that bank to secure its circulation?

Mr. GILFILLAN. Not in bonds. The excess was covered by United States notes deposited in the Treasury.

Senator BECK. I will come to that directly. It never had more than $500,000 of bonds at any one time, even when it had $852,550 of its notes outstanding?

Mr. GILFILLAN. That is all it was required to have. I do not think it had more.

Senator BECK. Therefore the only surety for the other $400,000 was legal-tender notes of the United States on deposit?

Mr. GILFILLAN. Yes, sir.

Senator BECK. There was no margin of 10 per cent. or any other per cent. deposited with the Treasurer for that amount of currency?

Senator KERNAN. The legal-tenders are par.

The CHAIRMAN. But there was no margin?

Mr. GILFILLAN. There was no margin except on that portion covered by United States bonds.

Senator BECK. Was there any other security for the $400,000 of the notes of this bank in excess of the $450,000 borne upon its books, except the legal-tender notes of the United States?

Mr. GILFILLAN. There was not.

Senator BECK. Do you understand that that was a compliance with the spirit of the law which required bonds of, say, $100,000 for every $90,000 of currency that was issued, or was it not a violation of the spirit of that law merely to have legal-tender notes and no bonds deposited?

Mr. GILFILLAN. It was in compliance with the construction placed upon the 4th section of the act of June 20th, 1874, which it is now contemplated to repeal.

Senator BECK. Section 5 of this bill proposes to repeal that and to restore sections 5159 and 5160 of the Revised Statutes. If that is done, will not each bank that seeks to retire its circulation have to deposit its own notes instead of greenbacks, and thus make that condition of things impossible?

Mr. GILFILLAN. That would be the effect.

Senator BECK. Is not that a safer system than the system that you have set forth in the illustration you have given of the operations of this bank on pages 20 and 21 of your report? Safer for the depositors, safer for the stockholders, and it prevents all this operation of your printing large quantities of notes at the expense of the United States, or of the other banks, for people who see fit to gamble in stocks and bonds?

Mr. GILFILLAN. It would be more economical for the United States.

Senator BECK. Is it not safer for the stockholders as well, and for the depositors, to have bonds of the United States always to the amount ?

Mr. GILFILLAN. It would be for the interest of the stockholders without doubt, to the extent of the margin on the bonds and premium over and above the amount of the circulating notes outstanding.

Senator MORRILL. Does not that depend upon the fact whether the United States notes become depreciated in value so as to be worth less than a hundred cents on the dollar ?

Mr. GILFILLAN. The value of the notes deposited is out of the question.

Senator MORRILL. If the United States notes are worth one hundred cents on the dollar then the security is good, is it not ?

Mr. GILFILLAN. It is good for the note-holder, but Senator Beck speaks of the stockholders of the bank.

Senator BECK. It is simply good, dollar for dollar, to the note-holder, but it is not as good as a United States bond at par would be, when there is only 90 per cent. of circulation represented by that bond.

Senator ALLISON. If instead of $90,000, you had $1,500,000 of bonds deposited and a margin of 50 per cent., would not the stockholders be still better off ?

Senator KERNAN. The stockholders would not get much dividends, but the creditors would be better off.

The CHAIRMAN. As I understand Mr. Beck's question it is very full of meaning (there is no doubt about that; it is one that has suggested itself to my mind before), that under the operation of a law that was intended to permit of elasticity in the volume of currency there can be worked a wholesale substitution of the security for the national-bank currency. Under the present banking act, the general act, the notes delivered to the banks for their circulation were secured by a deposit of bonds ten per cent. in excess of the face amount of the notes. They were secured by the liability of the stockholders for the amount of their subscriptions. They were secured by the reserve kept in the bank under the banking act; but when a bank not able or willing to procure its own circulating notes originally delivered to it by the Treasury shall take an equal number of United States notes and deposit them, then you have a substitution of an equal number of United States notes for the national-bank currency without any of the security offered by the ten per cent. excess of the bank, the liability of the stockholder, or the reserve required to be kept in the bank. That is the effect.

Senator BECK. That is the whole case.

The CHAIRMAN. That is the whole working of this law, and the question is whether or not it needs amendment.

Senator ALLISON. I want to make a suggestion. Is there not a confusion of terms in this, that these United States notes are not held at all as security, but they are the absolute redemption of those outstanding ?

Senator MORRILL. And in advance ?

Senator ALLISON. And in advance really ; because the national bank says: "Instead of paying out to A. B. and C. D., who hold my notes, I redeem these notes absolutely, according to law, by depositing the money in the Treasury"; and A. B. and C. D. go to the Treasury for their redemption, and not to the bank itself. So that the notes outstanding, for which United States notes are deposited in the Treasury, are not notes of the bank at all. They are notes that are practically redeemed by the bank, and in the Treasury.

Senator MORRILL. And which might have been redeemed from each individual holder.

The CHAIRMAN. They are paid by a promise to pay; they are paid by paper which is arbitrarily made a compulsory legal tender, and has not a cent of value in itself.

Senator ALLISON. Undoubtedly; but suppose a bank, instead of paying greenbacks into the Treasury, shall put gold eagles into the Treasury.

The CHAIRMAN. Then that is payment.

Senator ALLISON. That is redemption. Then we come back to a question of terms as to whether the greenback is money or not. If Mr. Beck is raising that question with you, that is another thing.

The CHAIRMAN. I am very glad to have the question brought right to that point.

Senator ALLISON. If the greenbacks are not money, then Mr. Beck is right.

The CHAIRMAN. Greenbacks are not money; they are nothing but a promise to pay money. My idea is that payment means payment and not a promise of payment.

Senator BECK. My whole object in questioning the Treasurer is because I am one of those who believe that the House acted wisely in repealing the section under which these possibilities exist and restoring sections 5159 and 5160 of the Revised Statutes, which require the banks to deposit their own notes themselves instead of requiring us to print new notes, up and down, and keep out double the amount of their currency only secured by anything, in violation of the law, and also which requires them to keep bonds to the amount of one-third of the circulation, and to repeal that provision, which reduces the bonds down to $50,000, as in the notable case of the Bank of Missouri, where it had two million and a half of capital, and ought to have had, and would have had, under sections 5159 and 5160, $833,000 of bonds, and yet when it failed it only had $50,000, and its stockholders and its depositors and everybody else suffered because of the construction of the act of 1874. I want to make these things impossible, and I am questioning the Treasurer to see whether or not in his opinion a repeal of that section and the restoration of the other sections would not be safer for depositors, stockholders, and the business of the country generally. Mr. Knox having given a judgment against it, I want to know if the Treasurer does not give his opinion in favor of the 5th section. I want to ask him the question now, whether he thinks section 5, repealing section 4 of the act of June 20, 1874, and sections 5159 and 5160, would not be a safe and wise provision to make.

Mr. GILFILLAN. I believe that the re-enactment of sections 5159 and 5160 would be for the benefit of the stockholders, and would facilitate refunding the debt. So far as the business of the Treasury is concerned, I am in favor of the repeal of the 4th section of the act of June 20, 1874, because it causes useless expense to the government and tends to derange the circulation of the country.

Senator KERNAN. And the re-enactment of the two sections named?

Mr. GILFILLAN. Yes, sir.

Senator ALLISON. What relation has the repeal of the 4th section and the substitution of the two other sections to the question of funding the public debt, if any?

Mr. GILFILLAN. The repeal of the 4th section of the act of June 20, 1874, would facilitate funding by retarding the withdrawal of bonds held as security for circulating notes and preventing a possible sudden contraction of the currency.

Senator ALLISON. It is a mere regulation of the Treasury for the convenience of the Treasurer?

Mr. GILFILLAN. The re-enactment of sections 5159 and 5160, of course, forbids the reduction of the amount of United States bonds on deposit in the Treasury below one-third of the capital of the national banks.

Senator ALLISON. Do you think it would have any effect one way or the other upon the refunding process under this proposed law?

Mr. GILFILLAN. By increasing the amount of bonds to be kept on deposit in the Treasury by national banks beyond the amount to which they may now reduce, as existing law is now interpreted, it is an aid to refunding.

Senator ALLISON. And, so far as it is a compulsory process, if the bonds should fall below par it would then find a market for that number, whatever it would be.

Mr. GILFILLAN. Yes, sir; but I do not suppose Congress would desire to compel national banks to take a bond below par.

Senator WALLACE. They could only be compelled to take about sixty millions of dollars, as I understood the Comptroller of the Currency day before yesterday.

Senator ALLISON. Do you think it would be wise or unwise to make a provision here which would operate compulsorily upon any portion of the people with reference to taking the bonds.

Mr. GILFILLAN. In that view of it, it might be unwise to compel the banks to hold any particular class of bonds.

Senator BECK. I forgot to ask a question of the Secretary of the Treasury when he was here, when something was said about the rate of interest on English consols ranging for the last twenty-five years from an average of about $3\frac{1}{4}$ to $3\frac{1}{2}$, as a reason for supposing that we could not refund at 3 per cent. Do you know whether the English consols are subject to taxation, and whether incomes in England, derived from consols, are also taxed as well as any others?

Mr. GILFILLAN. No, sir; I have not looked into that subject.

I wish to say in regard to the remark of Senator Wallace, that, as the law now stands interpreted by the Department of Justice, the national banks can reduce the bonds in the hands of the Treasurer of the United States as security for circulation to $60,000,000, but with the re-enactment of those two sections they could not reduce below $152,500,000.

Senator WALLACE. But taking the 5th section as it stands here, and making a compulsory market for the bonds that are to be treated as the bonds in which we refund our debt, I understood the Comptroller to say that we could only make a compulsory market to-day for about $60,000,000?

Mr. GILFILLAN. As the 5th section stands you can compel them to keep all they have and to hold the present amount of bonds, which is $359,000,000, unless reduced by the cancellation of circulating notes.

Senator MORRILL. Could you compel those who have $4\frac{1}{2}$'s on deposit?

Mr. GILFILLAN. I do not suppose that is the intention of the 5th section.

Senator WALLACE. That is the point exactly. I understood the Comptroller very clearly to say that a compulsory market for only $60,000,000 could be made under the 5th section. Therefore you could compel the national banks to surrender the whole of their bonds to what extent and take the 3's?

Mr. GILFILLAN. I had not looked at it in that light; but it will certainly compel them to have of United States bonds the present amount for the time being, until reduced by cancellation of circulation.

Senator WALLACE. I have no doubt of that.

Mr. GILFILLAN. If those two sections are not re-enacted, they need have but $60,000,000 in bonds of any kind on deposit. I do not suppose that the 5th section would compel them absolutely to withdraw all their bonds and replace them with the new bonds.

Senator BECK. The 4½'s of 1891, and the 4's of 1907 you cannot compel them to take.

Mr. GILFILLAN. I think it is not compulsory as to bonds now on deposit.

Senator WALLACE. Only as those bonds become due and can be called. If they continue their circulation, they must deposit 3 per cents and 3 per cents alone?

Mr. GILFILLAN. I suppose if banks wish to exchange the bonds on deposit for others, they must exchange them for the new bonds.

Senator ALLISON. That is, the process going on now could not go on except for new bonds.

Mr. GILFILLAN. I suppose that is the effect of the 5th section.

Senator MORRILL. Under the existing laws as they have been, there does not seem to be much disposition on the part of the whole country to increase the stock of national banks. Do you suppose that passing the 5th section would have a tendency to induce people to embark more largely their capital in national banks, or would it diminish the amount that is already there?

Mr. GILFILLAN. I suppose that would depend more on the status of the bonds in the market and the state of business than anything else.

The CHAIRMAN. In the process of depositing United States notes and the withdrawal of United States bonds by a bank, leaving the notes originally issued to such bank still outstanding, is there any possibility of an increase in the volume of currency?

Mr. GILFILLAN. Not in that operation; not in that one transaction.

The CHAIRMAN. I have reference to the process.

Mr. GILFILLAN. Of course you do not refer now to the national-bank circulation? In speaking of an increase of circulation you refer to the circulation of the country, not of the national-bank notes?

The CHAIRMAN. The volume of paper currency, that which consists of United States notes and what are termed national-bank notes. I want to know whether, by the proceedings which you referred to and described in your report, of depositing United States notes for the purpose of taking up bonds which were originally placed there as security for the notes issued to the banks, there is any possibility by that process of expanding the volume of the paper currency?

Senator MORRILL. In the aggregate?

The CHAIRMAN. In the aggregate.

Mr. GILFILLAN. No, sir; not in the aggregate.

The CHAIRMAN. It would seem there was none, to me, but I thought I would ask you as an expert upon that subject.

Mr. GILFILLAN. No, sir; it has not occurred.

Senator BECK. Is it not possible, on the other hand, to the extent that the national banks hold greenbacks in their possession, that they could, if it was their interest, deposit simultaneously the amount of greenbacks that they have, whether it was one or two hundred millions, withdraw their bonds, and contract their circulation to that extent in a day?

Mr. GILFILLAN. Yes, sir.

Senator BECK. But if they had to collect their own notes and bring them in, they would have to do it much more slowly?

Mr. GILFILLAN. Yes; it would be more gradual.

Senator ALLISON. But could they not under that same process gather up their notes and at a given day do the same thing?

Mr. GILFILLAN. Yes, sir.

Senator MORRILL. Is it dependent solely upon the amount of funds that they have to loan? Is there any sort of danger or apprehension in any quarter that they will ever do that for the simple purpose of contracting the currency?

Mr. GILFILLAN. Either process might become detrimental to the public interests. Existing law makes both possible. The fifth section will prevent excessive contraction by deposit of United States notes, and leaves redundant bank circulation to gradually find its way back to the banks by the natural process of being voluntarily surrendered by the holders to the Treasury for redemption.

Senator MORRILL. But my point is, whether a bank which depends upon loaning its capital, its bills, such as it has on hand, would be likely to put them out of its hands where it could not loan them?

Mr. GILFILLAN. No, sir; the only way they could get them back would be to sell the bonds. They would lose the use of their funds temporarily and suffer loss of interest, possibly.

The committee adjourned.

www.ingramcontent.com/pod-product-compliance
Lightning Source LLC
Chambersburg PA
CBHW021533270326
41930CB00008B/1231